Lookout Cookbook

A Collection of Recipes by Forest Fire Lookouts Throughout the United States

Libby Langston

P.O. Box 812
Coeur D'Alene, Idaho 83816-0812
(208) 664-3448
ISBN 0-9723356-5-X.
10 9 8 7 6 5 4 3 2 1

Layout and design, computerized image enhancement
and production by:

Moore Graphics Studio
30217 Corte Plata
Temecula, California 92591
smoore10@adelphia.net

Libby Langston
Missoula, Montana
libbylan@bigsky.net

Printed on 60# Opaque White by Sheridan Books

Book typeset in Papyrus, Stone Serif, Lucida Sans Bold and Times
using QuarkXPress.

Cover art and chapter partitions:
Tom Reul

Back cover photograph:
Mary Lou Mills

Dedication page and page facing Table of Contents:
Miss Helen Dowe on duty at Devil's Head Lookout,
Pike National Forest, Colorado- July 15, 1919

DEDICATION

This cookbook is dedicated to
all Forest Fire Lookouts.

RECOGNITION

This book was produced through a cooperative venture between the Idaho/Montana Chapter of the Forest Fire Lookout Association (FFLA), the Lolo National Forest of the USDA Forest Service and the Museum of North Idaho.

Special thanks go to the Blackfoot Forest Protective Association for initial funding and to all the lookouts and their loved ones who submitted recipes and photographs.

Thanks also go to Cindy Holder and Kathy Johnson for their assistance, support and encouragement throughout the project.

ABOUT THIS BOOK

My first experience at a lookout tower involved hiking nine miles to the top of a peak on the Clearwater National Forest in Idaho to visit a friend who had escaped the city to be a lookout. Upon my approach to the tower, she waved to me from the catwalk outside her cozy little summer home on its very tall legs. After climbing the four flights of steps to the cabin, she greeted me with bread she had baked that morning. Because of this unforgettable trip in 1985, I've been drawn to lookouts.

Over time I've visited friends working lookouts, I've occasionally filled in for a lookout and I often rent lookouts. My love for lookouts drove me to create a book that would honor the people who are lookouts and foster appreciation for the structures themselves. My hope is that this book, *The Lookout Cookbook*, will raise awareness of these historic structures and help raise money to restore more lookouts throughout the United States.

Libby Langston and her dog Khirbi at West Fork Butte Lookout in Montana (2003)

Table of Contents

Lookout Tree on Horse Butte Point, Gallatin National Forest, Montana
By Tom Reul

Breakfast

Breakfast before going on duty at Little Guard Lookout on the Coeur d'Alene National Forest (1959)

Indian Mountain Pancakes

John Agars, 17 seasons (1984-2000)
Indian Mountain Lookout (LO)
Kaniksu National Forest
Washington

Indian Mountain Lookout on the Kaniksu National Forest

3 heaping Tbsp. pancake mix (preferably Snoqualmie Falls brand)

2 heaping Tbsp. yogurt (plain or vanilla...fruit flavor okay if huckleberries are not in season)

1 egg or 2-3 spoonfuls of Egg Beaters brand

1 spoonful cooking oil (olive or other)

1/2 cup or so of fresh huckleberries (must be picked 5 minutes before using)

Water to make proper consistency (don't make too runny)

Mix all ingredients except oil. Heat up frying pan. Use spoonful of oil in pan to get crisp, crunchy edges. Cook slowly and watch for bubbles. When eight or ten bubbles don't close anymore, it's time to flip. Second side cooks more quickly.

Makes 2 good-sized pancakes and leaves enough for one smaller pancake for your loyal Golden Retriever, hiking companion, and guest-greeter.

"Nice quiet indoor work with no heavy lifting (of course that does not apply when you have to hike up to the lookout from the closest trailhead 600 feet below). Of course, it is great to spend the summer in a government-owned penthouse with a fantastic view! And, they even pay you $60.00 a week!"

— John Agars

Francie and John Agars shared the lookout job at Indian Mountain Lookout in 1991. (Photo taken in 1984—John's first season)

Overnighter's Breakfast

Susan (Parsons) Holland, 4 seasons (1985-1988)
Bear Mountain LO, Rocky Point LO,
Beaver Ridge LO
Clearwater National Forest
Idaho
Huckleberry Lookout
Willamette National Forest
Oregon

Bear Mountain Lookout is an 8-mile hike from Jerry Johnson Hot Springs. (1985)

potatoes, sliced or cubed
onions
broccoli
green peppers
garlic
mushrooms
salt and pepper to taste
cheese (optional)

Susan (Parsons) Holland cooking at Rocky Point Lookout in Idaho (1986)

Cook potatoes in a skillet with oil until almost soft. Add any or all of the vegetables. When vegetables are cooked to desired level, top with grated cheese, if available, and cover to melt. Serve with chopped green onions, black olives, avocados, diced tomatoes or alfalfa sprouts on top. Put salsa or sour cream on the side.

Note: As with any lookout recipe, substitution is the norm.

"A great place to get in touch with your emotions."
— Susan Parsons Holland

Helen McCrain at Summit Point Lookout (1991)

Quinoa (Keen-wah) Hot Cereal

Helen McCrain, 2 seasons (1991-1992)
Summit Point Lookout
Wallowa-Whitman National Forest
Oregon

1 cup Quinoa
2 cups water
pinch of salt
milk
honey

Rinse Quinoa, cover with cold water, swirl and drain thoroughly. Bring water to a boil, add Quinoa and return to a boil. Simmer covered for 15 minutes. Remove from heat; cover and let stand for 10 minutes. Fluff with a fork (it cooks like rice) and add milk and honey to taste.

Serve hot with fruit or juice and toast.

"Quinoa was a primary food of Native Americans over 5,000 years ago. The Inca Civilization used it as a staple food."

— Helen McCrain

Perfection Omelet

From "The Lookout Cookbook, Region One" (1938)
submitted by Dave Slagle, 3 seasons (1939-41)
Columbia Mountain LO, Fir Mountain LO
Colville National Forest
Washington

David Slagle at Fir Mountain Lookout (1940)

3 eggs
3 tsp. cornstarch (scant)
1/2 tsp. baking powder
1/2 cup milk
salt and pepper to taste
cheese or cooked ham or bacon

Beat egg yolks. Add cornstarch dissolved with a little milk. Add rest of milk and salt and pepper. Beat egg whites stiff. Add baking powder. Blend all together. Pour into hot, greased skillet and bake 20-30 minutes in moderate oven. Chopped, crisp bacon, cooked ham, or cheese may be used in omelet.

"Summer usually ends with a bang on a lookout. The end of August brings the Fall Equinox and a challenge to your courage. Tales of direct hits by lightning on lookouts are in the back of your mind. Mid-August 1941, on Fir Mountain, brought the worst storm I was to experience. I saw at least 10 smokes on the adjoining ridge, my telephone went down, rocks sprayed the station. The storm was under me, over me, and deafening—lightning almost constant and terrifyng. Mt. Annie and I got it about the same. Ralph Brashears and I should have been awarded Silver Stars for surviving that one! Floyd Cory gave me 7 days off instead. I was 20 years old, and was most impressed with the fury of the mountain.

St. Elmo's fire is a phenomenon peculiar to towers with lightning rods. A lookout tower is equipped with an assortment of cables; the individual wires are fanned out on the point of the roof, and they are drilled into the rocks at the base of the tower and cemented in place. They are designed to ground a direct hit from lightning, and probably work most of the time. But when a storm cloud approaches, these cables turn a bluish-white neon color. They definitely glow. It is particularly disturbing at night, when you are awakened by a thunderclap. This one storm hung around for 6 to 7 hours and old St. Elmo practically wore those cables out!"

— Dave Slagle

Beaver Ridge Lookout (1996)
(Photo by Byron Bonney)

Spam Delight

Chuck Kjell Petersen, 6 seasons
(1968, 1996, 1998-2001)
Snow Peak Lookout
St. Joe National Forest
Beaver Ridge Lookout
Clearwater National Forest
Idaho

Spam
graham crackers
sweetened applesauce

Lightly fry sliced Spam. (Being careful not to get 2nd degree burns from spattering grease. I suggest being fully clothed during this step!) Place fried Spam slices between graham crackers to form a sandwich. Serve with a large bowl of sweetened applesauce.

Exercise vigorously after eating to prevent cardiac death.

"In 1968 I didn't give much thought to diet or what the health factors might be of what I ate. I accidentally stumbled on my Spam Delight breakfast, ate it nearly every morning and have never touched the stuff again!"

— Chuck Kjell Petersen

Blue Huckleberry and Kinnikinnik Jam

Shannon and Joey Hodgson
8 seasons (1997-2004)
Hickman Butte LO, Sisi LO
Mt. Hood National Forest
Oregon

Shannon and Joey Hodgson have an unspoiled view of Mount Hood from Hickman Butte LO. (2004)

2 cups crushed blue huckleberries
2 cups crushed Kinnikinnik berries
1 package of pectin
3 cups of sugar

First, wash and boil jars (sterilize). Bring berries and pectin to a boil in a saucepan. Then, add sugar. Boil for one minute, constantly stirring. Pour into jars; put on lids and rings. Then, boil all jars of jam in a big pan full of water for 10 minutes. Remove jars from pan and set on a towel. If jars do not seal, refrigerate and use first. Makes about 6 1/2 pints.

We have picked a lot of wild berries and made jam with them. Our most exotic and out of the ordinary recipe is this one.

"The other day when we were in the middle of our jam-making project, a storm rolled over us. First, we were hit with a downpour of rain and wind, then the thunder and lightning showed up. We turned off our stove and jumped on our glass-legged stool. My husband called dispatch and went out of service, turned off the radio and returned to the stool. Fortunately, it was a quick storm and we were able to return to our jam project."

— Shannon Hodgson

Rosanne Davis at Saddle Mountain Lookout (1992)

Tummy Warmer

Rosanne Davis, 3 seasons
(1992-1994)
Saddle Mountain Lookout
Department of State Lands
Montana

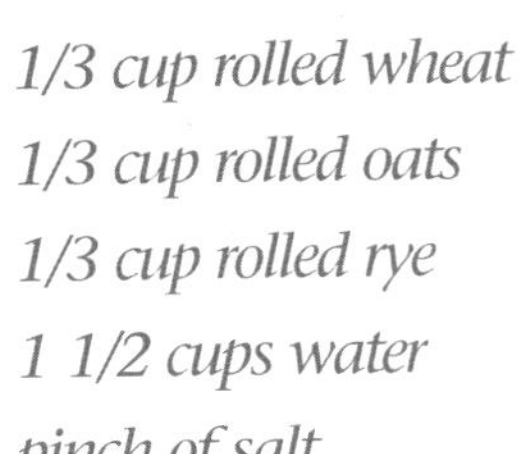

1/3 cup rolled wheat
1/3 cup rolled oats
1/3 cup rolled rye
1 1/2 cups water
pinch of salt

Bring to a boil. Lower heat to a simmer. Add chopped dry food (apricots, bananas, papaya, pineapple, huckleberries, dates).

Cook covered for 10 minutes.

Optional topping of chopped nuts or milk.

"Beyond having become a lightning junkie...I loved getting up with the sun, going to bed when it went down, the comings and goings of animal and plant life, living part of the natural rhythm of nature."

— Rosanne Davis

Saddle Mountain lookout was built by the Blackfoot Cattleman's Association in 1943.

Scrapple

From "The Lookout Cookbook, Region One" (1938)
submitted by Dave Slagle, 3 seasons (1939-41)
Columbia Mountain LO, Fir Mountain LO
Colville National Forest
Washington

1/2 lb. bacon

3/4 cup cornmeal

1 tsp. onion juice

2 cups water

1 tsp. salt

2 Tbsp. minced parsley (optional)

Chop bacon. Fry lightly. Boil water and add cornmeal. Add bacon and seasonings. Cook over low heat until very thick, stirring constantly. Place in loaf pan. Chill overnight. Cover with waxed paper to keep crust from forming. Cut into thin slices. Dip in flour or beaten egg and crumbs and fry in hot skillet. For a complete meal, serve with scrambled eggs and fried apple slices.

Columbia Mountain Lookout (1939)

"Floyd Cory made me a lookout in July 1939 when a Forestry student from the University of Michigan became ill and had to be replaced. At 18 years of age, I was to be a temporary, and only for 3 to 4 days. But, I finished the season when the Michiganer decided he could not return to the isolation of Columbia Mountain.

I had little fresh food, at first, until my dad and brother Maury backpacked fresh supplies and a battery radio in for company. The first sounds from that radio announced that Hitler had invaded Poland. The radio and Tony Gilman, on White Mountain, were my companions for the rest of that season." —Dave Slagle

Dave's reliable companion (1939)

Ninemile Lookout was one of several lookouts Myrl McKenna built and occupied. This one was built in 1932-33.

Jellies

from Myrl McKenna's 1933
Daily Log and Diary
Ninemile Lookout
Lolo National Forest
Montana

Peach Butter

Peel peaches. Cook in as little water as possible, without burning, until mushy. Add 1/2 as much sugar as pulp. Cook until thick and clear. Add spices. Seal while hot.

Blackberry Jam

Mash berries. Cook in own juice until hot. Press through sieve to remove seeds. Add one cup of sugar per pint of juice. Cook rapidly until thick. Pack in hot jars and seal with paraffin or lids.

"July 1929: (while building Bear Gulch LO)

6 Tuesday–cut and cary (sic) poles for floor of the tower. Moved map board from old to the new tower. Air patrol past at 10:20 a.m. Freese out fire burning big"

— Excerpt from Myrl McKenna's "IDEAS" book

Myrl McKenna with Rosie the Mule (1933)

Myrl McKenna drew cartoons on every page of his Daily Log and Diary while working the Ninemile Lookout in 1933.

(Historical Museum at Fort Missoula–Kenneth C. McKenna collection)

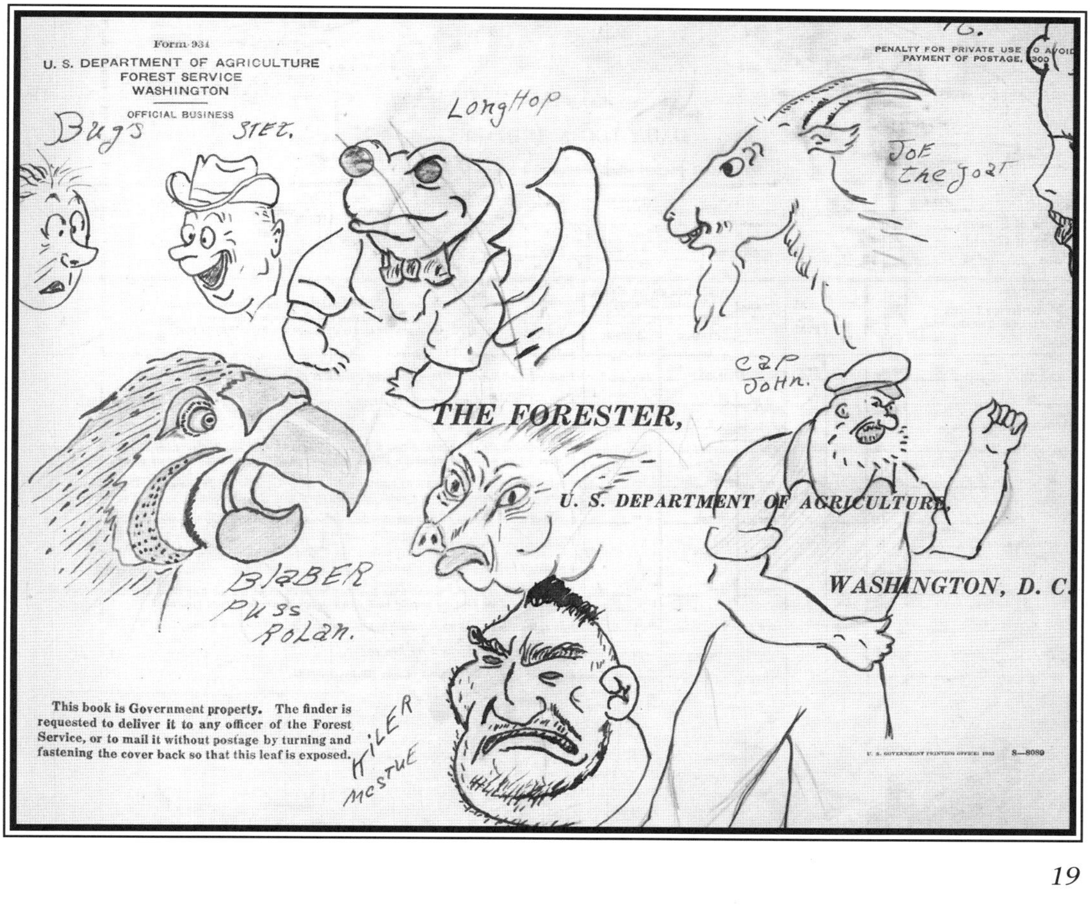

Form 934
U. S. DEPARTMENT OF AGRICULTURE
FOREST SERVICE
WASHINGTON

OFFICIAL BUSINESS

PENALTY FOR PRIVATE USE TO AVOID PAYMENT OF POSTAGE, $300

Bugs   Stet.   LongHop   Joe the goat

cap John.

THE FORESTER,

U. S. DEPARTMENT OF AGRICULTURE,

WASHINGTON, D. C.

Blaber   Puss   Rolan.

This book is Government property. The finder is requested to deliver it to any officer of the Forest Service, or to mail it without postage by turning and fastening the cover back so that this leaf is exposed.

Hiler McStue

S—8089

Hidden Peak Syrup

Rolly (Sam) Grotte, 5 seasons
(1951-54 & 1995)
Bear Mountain LO, Hidden Peak LO,
Roundtop LO, Beaver Ridge LO
Clearwater National Forest
Idaho

Sam standing on the catwalk at Bear Mountain LO (1995)

1 1/2 cups sugar
1 cup water
1 tsp. maple flavor
1/2 tsp. vanilla, rum, or almond (my favorite) flavor

Heat to boiling point and be sure sugar is dissolved.

"There aren't a lot of days on lookout of absolute calm, but they are memorable when they occur. Temperatures may run into the 80's even at altitudes above 8000 feet. Bees make enough noise in their search for flowers that they can be heard on the tower catwalk and flying ants arrive in the thousands to mate on every centimeter of lookout window and structure. With this company, who can say it's lonesome on lookout?"

— Sam Grotte

Good Morning Pancakes

Rosanne Davis, 3 seasons (1992-1994)
Saddle Mountain Lookout
Department of State Lands
Montana

Saddle Mountain Lookout is managed by the Montana Department of State Lands, now called the Montana Department of Natural Resources. (1992)

2 cups white rice (leftover from dinner)

1 egg

1/2 tsp. flour

1 tsp. sugar

salt and pepper to taste

Mix ingredients and form into a patty. Cook in a buttered skillet over medium heat until cooked thoroughly.

"For entertainment I highly recommend National Public Radio's "Selected Shorts" program. Reception was clearer on the mountain than in the Missoula Valley. There is nothing like snuggling into bed, turning down the lantern and having someone read stories to you while the tower sways in the wind."

— Rosanne Davis

Nub Lookout, Clearwater National Forest, Idaho
By Tom Reul

Mrs. Hollis Stritch hauls water to her lookout on West Fork Butte in western Montana in 1943. (Photo by K.D. Swan)

Miss Christine's Southern Style Corn Bread

Shelton Lewis, 3 seasons (1989-91)
Clear Springs Fire Tower
Bienville National Forest
Mississippi

Shelton Lewis with Christine Harris at the Clear Springs Fire Tower, located just above the Clear Springs Baptist Church. After Sunday services, Christine would look up to the tower to see if any shadowy figures could be spotted. If so, she would have two or three young boys deliver a hot meal from the church to the lookout on duty. Shelton was the lucky recipient of these meals many times. Christine Harris' corn bread is the quintessential addition to any fine southern meal.

1 cup white corn meal

1/2 tsp. baking soda

1/2 tsp. table salt

1 egg, beat well

1 cup buttermilk

1 tsp. shortening (Christine prefers vegetable oil)

Sift dry ingredients together. Mix egg and buttermilk and add to the dry ingredients. Add shortening and pour into a greased shallow pan. Bake in a very hot 450 degree oven for 18 minutes. Serves about six people.

"If you use self-rising corn meal, do not add the baking soda and salt. One more important note from Christine Harris: 'NEVER PUT SUGAR IN SOUTHERN CORN BREAD!' "

— Shelton Lewis

Middle Fork Peak Muffins

Alexia Cochrane, 8 seasons
(1976, 77, 80, 81, 86-88, 90)
Lookout Mtn LO, Bad Luck LO, Elkhorn LO,
Long Tom LO, Middle Fork Peak LO,
Coolwater LO
Bitterroot National Forest
Salmon National Forest
Nez Perce National Forest
Montana and Idaho

Middle Fork Peak Lookout is located at 9200 feet within Idaho's Salmon National Forest. (1988)

Preheat oven to 375 degrees.

In a large bowl, mix:

1 cup whole wheat flour
1 cup unbleached flour
1 Tbsp. baking powder
1/4 tsp. salt
1 tsp. cinnamon
1/2 cup raisins
1/2 cup walnuts (optional)

> ***"This recipe was created on Middle Fork Lookout in 1987. These are really good muffins... I still staff lookouts as needed during big fire years."***
>
> ***— Alexia Cochrane***

Stir in 1 1/2 cups shredded carrots.

In a separate bowl, mix:

1/2 cup honey
2/3 cup milk
1/4 cup oil (substitute 1/2 cup apple sauce for low fat muffins)
1 tsp. vanilla
1 egg

Alexia Cochrane's catch from a lake near Middle Fork Peak Lookout

Add to dry ingredients and gently blend together. Bake in greased muffin tin 40-45 minutes.

English Muffin Bread

Milicent Furrer, 5 seasons (1990's)
Anthony Peak Lookout
Mendocino National Forest
California

Anthony Peak LO is located on the second highest mountain in Mendocino County, California at 6954 feet.

(makes one loaf)

1 pkt. (1 Tbsp.) yeast
3 cups unsifted flour
1/2 Tbsp. sugar
1 tsp. salt
1 cup milk
1/8 tsp. baking soda
1/4 cup water
small amount of corn meal

Combine half of flour, the yeast, sugar, salt and baking soda. Heat liquids until very warm (do not boil!). Add to dry mixture and beat well. Stir in rest of flour to make a stiff batter. Spoon into a loaf pan that has been greased and sprinkled with cornmeal. Sprinkle top with cornmeal. Cover and let rise in warm place for 45 minutes. Bake at 400 degrees for 25 minutes or so. Remove from pan immediately and cool.

"Makes a great bread for garlic bread. When toasted, this bread tastes just like English muffins."

— Milicent Furrer

Cinnamon Rolls

From "The Lookout Cookbook, Region One" (1954)
Mitchel R. White and Linda J. White Trifaro
7 seasons (1980's & 1990's)
Saddle Mountain Lookout
Gila National Forest
Arizona

Saddle Mountain Lookout is located at 8340 feet on the Gila National Forest. (1986)

Dough

2 Tbsp. sugar

2 Tbsp. melted shortening

1 beaten egg

3/4 tsp. salt

1 cup lukewarm liquid (1/2 cup milk, 1/2 cup water)

3 cups sifted flour

1 yeast cake (1 Tbsp. or pkt. powdered yeast)

Combine all except shortening, which is added after half the flour. Knead until smooth. Let rise until twice its size.

"Part your heavens, O Lord, and come down; touch the mountains, so that they may smoke." Psalm 144:5

Cinnamon Filling

1 1/2 tsp. cinnamon

1/3 cup butter

1/2 cup brown sugar

1/2 cup chopped nuts (your choice)

Turn dough on floured board and roll out to 1-inch thickness. Spread with melted butter, sprinkle with sugar, cinnamon, and nuts. Roll dough up into a round cylinder-shaped roll, and cut into 1-inch slices. Place in well-greased pan and let rise to double their size. Brush tops with melted shortening and bake in moderate oven for approximately 20 minutes (350-400 degrees).

Indian Mountain Huckleberry Coffee Cake

John Agars, 17 seasons (1984-2000)
Indian Mountain Lookout
Kaniksu National Forest
Washington

John Agars' daughter, Annie, worked the lookout with him in 1984-85.

Crumble Topping

1/2 cup sugar
1/2 cup flour
1/2 tsp. cinnamon
1/4 cup butter

Combine ingredients and mix until crumbly. Set aside.

Cake

1/4 cup shortening
1 1/4 cup sugar
2 eggs
2 cups sifted flour
1/2 tsp. salt
1 tsp. baking powder
3/4 cup milk
1 1/2 tsp. vanilla
1 Tbsp. grated orange rind
1 cup huckleberries

Cream shortening and sugar. Beat in eggs one at a time. Sift flour, salt, baking powder. Add to creamed mixture alternately with milk, blending after each addition. Stir in vanilla and orange rind. Fold in berries. Pour into a 9-inch square greased pan.

Sprinkle with crumble topping. Bake at 350 degrees for 45-50 minutes. Serves 9.

Betsy's Bowman Lake Bran Muffins

Betsy Spettigue, 2 seasons (1980-81)
Numa Lookout
Glacier National Park
Montana

Numa Lookout (1981)

In one bowl:

3 cups All Bran Cereal, Bran Flakes or Bran or any combination of all three

1 cup boiling water (poured over bran)

In a second larger bowl, mix:

2 cups low-fat buttermilk

1 cup sugar (can use honey or fructose–quantity to taste)

1/2 cup oil (safflower best)

2 eggs

Betsy Spettigue straining drinking water at Numa Lookout (1981)

Stir thoroughly, then add:

2 1/4 cups whole wheat flour

1/2 cup soy flour (refrigerate after opening!)

1/2 cup oat bran (Mother's brand is best)

2 tsp. baking soda

Stir in bran from first bowl. Bake at 350 degrees for 15 minutes or so. Makes 2 dozen.

Can make 2 dozen at once and freeze or make them in the morning–just refrigerate muffin mix!

"One of the finest outhouse views I've ever experienced!"

— Betsy Spettigue

George Rosenbalm on his 56th birthday on Table Rock Lookout (September 3, 1986)

Sourdough Starter and Biscuits

George Rosenbalm, 7 seasons (1986-1992)
Table Rock LO, Lookout Mountain,
Spout Springs LO, High Ridge LO
Umatilla National Forest
Oregon & Washington

Sourdough Starter

2 cups flour

1 package dry yeast

2 cups warm water

Mix with wooden spoon. Cover bowl (glass or pottery—NOT metal) with a dishcloth or paper towel and let stand for 48-72 hours. After starter has set for 3 days, put 1 cup in a glass or pottery jar, cover, and store in a cool place. The remaining starter can then be used for pancakes or bread.

"Most of my cookin' was by trial and error. I combined my mother-in-law's German recipes with sourdough sponge. Certain quirks of my methods may not be accepted by professional cooks, but they produce tasty, good results."

— George Rosenbalm

Biscuits

2 cups sourdough starter

1 cup milk or evaporated milk (sometimes I mix half & half)

3 eggs (room temperature)

1/3 cup oil

Blend the ingredients together and mix well. Now here comes the specialty...put 2 Tbsp. sugar in a small bowl. Add 1 tsp. baking soda (not powder). Add 1 tsp. salt. Stir and shake. Add to sourdough mixture. Cover and let the chemical reaction work for 30 minutes. Then add white enriched flour and knead to the proper texture. Place it back in the bowl, cover and let it rise for about an hour or more.

Six Thousand Foot English Muffins

Mary Byers, 9 seasons (1980's)
Sula Peak Lookout
Bitterroot National Forest
Montana

Mary Byers snapping to the music at Sula Peak in Montana (1987)

"With the absence of big worldly events, minutiae become the focus of your life-- a spider catching gnats, the growth of a plant, the degree of your tan." — Mary Byers

1 Tbsp. active dry yeast
1 cup water
1/2 cup milk
2 tsp. sugar
1 tsp. salt
3 Tbsp. softened butter
4 cups sifted flour (2 cups whole wheat, 2 cups unbleached sifted together)

In a mixing bowl, combine the water, milk, sugar and salt. Dissolve the yeast in 2 Tbsp. warm water for 3-5 minutes and then combine with the above ingredients.

Beat 2 cups flour gradually into the milk mixture. Cover with a cloth and let rise in a warm place for about 1 1/2 hours or until it collapses back into the bowl.

Beat in butter.

Beat or knead in the remaining flour.

Place the dough on a board lightly floured or sprinkled with cornmeal. Pat or press dough to a thickness of 1/2 inch. Cut into three-inch rounds. On a slightly greased sheet, let stand until doubled in size. With a spatula, carefully transfer to a fairly hot, well-buttered griddle. Cook both sides until light brown. Cool slightly on a rack.

To separate muffins before traditional toasting, take two forks back to back and pry them open horizontally.

Breadsticks

Chris Baker, 17 seasons (1988-2004)
Swiftcurrent LO, Huckleberry LO
Glacier National Park
Montana

Combine:

2 cups warm water

1 pkt. (1 Tbsp.) yeast

1 heaping Tbsp. sugar

Stir in:

1 cup flour

1 Tbsp. salt

Add:

4 more cups flour

Mix well, but not excessively. Let rise until double in size. Turn out on floured board (dough will be sticky) and pat into a large rectangle. Cut into strips. Place strips on a large cookie sheet or in a 9 X 13 pan and let rise a second time. Bake in 400-degree oven for 20 minutes. Brush or drizzle with garlic butter and salt lightly.

"Good for rainy, socked-in days".

— Chris Baker

A packstring delivers Chris Baker's supplies to Huckleberry Lookout in the 1990's.

Bear Mountain LO Whole Wheat Bread

Susan (Parsons) Holland, 4 seasons (1985-1988)
Bear Mountain LO, Rocky Point LO,
Beaver Ridge LO
Clearwater National Forest
Idaho
Huckleberry Lookout
Willamette National Forest
Oregon

A helicopter delivered Susan's monthly food supply to Bear Mountain LO. (1985)

Makes one loaf:

1 1/2 cups water

1 Tbsp. yeast

1/4 cup sweetening

1/2 cup dried milk

2 cups whole wheat flour (good if you add oatmeal and sesame seeds here)

This mixture will be muddy. Let rise.

> **"This is a good recipe for bread at a lookout using dry ingredients that you usually have on hand."**
>
> **— Susan Parsons Holland**

After rising, add:

1/2 Tbsp. salt

1/8 to 1/4 cup oil

1 1/2 to 2 cups whole wheat flour

Use one more cup of whole wheat flour to knead in.

Shape into loaf and place in bread pan.

Let rise.

Bake at 300 degrees in propane oven for about one hour (high altitude). Regular oven: Bake at 375 degrees for 40-45 minutes.

The "kitchen" in Bear Mountain LO (1985)

FMO's Favorite Apricot-Ginger Scones

Jodi Allison-Bunnell, 1 season (1992)
Table Rock Lookout
Umatilla National Forest
Washington

Table Rock Lookout (1992)

"It was a summer of peace that has shaped major parts of my life ever since. I wouldn't trade it for anything."

— Jodi Allison-Bunnell

1 cup white flour
1 cup whole wheat flour
1 tsp. cream of tartar
2 Tbsp. brown sugar
1 tsp. baking soda
1/4 tsp. salt
3 1/2 Tbsp. dried buttermilk
3 Tbsp. butter
1 cup plus two tablespoons water
2 Tbsp. chopped sugared gingerroot
1/2 cup chopped dried apricots

Blend dry ingredients together, then cut in butter with pastry blender. Stir in gingerroot and dried apricots; add water. Turn out onto flat surface. Roll into a circle 3/4" thick and slice into six or eight wedges. Bake on a flour-coated cookie sheet or pie pan until middle is done. Best served warm with butter to your visiting FMO (Fire Management Officer).

Bear Mountain Sourdough

Rolly (Sam) Grotte, 5 seasons (1951-54, 1995)
Bear Mountain LO, Hidden Peak LO
Roundtop LO, Beaver Ridge LO
Clearwater National Forest
Idaho

Bear Mountain Lookout (1995)

1/2 pkt. of yeast
1 cup warm water
2 to 3 cups flour
2 Tbsp. plus 1 tsp. sugar
pinch of salt
1 egg, beaten
1 Tbsp. butter, melted
milk
pinch of baking soda

In a glass, stoneware or plastic pot with a loose lid, mix yeast in a cup of warm water. Put 2 to 3 cups of flour in pot and mix with yeast water until you have a heavy, slightly lumpy, sticky dough. Cover lightly and leave in a warm (not hot) place for a day or two. The night before eating, add enough flour so that you'll have 2 cups of starter left over plus whatever amount you'll eat. Add warm water (or try warm milk) and 1 tsp. of sugar. Mix to the same heavy starter consistency. The next morning put starter in bowl (except for the 2 cups you leave in the starter pot.) Mix sugar, salt, egg, butter, baking soda and enough warm milk to make batter smooth. Allow to rise for 30 minutes or so. Use a heavy cast iron skillet or frying pan to cook. Best if used every day or two.

"Don't believe it when they say ' You can never go back.' I built (with 2 others) Bear Mountain Lookout in 1951. Forty-four years later, I returned to find only three changes: a radio replaced my faithful telephone, a wonderful propane refrigerator took the place of my screen cooler on the north side of the LO cabin, and a propane stove was nice when the oven didn't explode."

— Sam Grotte

Swan Hill/ Mission Lookout, Flathead National Forest, Montana
By Tom Reul

Stanley Lukens at Emerine Lookout located 19 miles southwest of Philipsburg, Montana (1929)

Hot Western Sandwiches

From "The Lookout Cookbook, Region One" (1954)
Missoula, Montana

Rock Rabbit Crow's Nest and log cabin were built in 1929 in what is now the Frank Church River of No Return Wilderness, Idaho.

4 slices bacon

1 Tbsp. chopped onion

2 Tbsp. chopped green pepper

4 eggs

1/4 cup milk

1/2 tsp. salt

Worcestershire sauce

Cook bacon until crisp. Lightly brown onion and green pepper in fat.
Beat eggs with milk and seasonings. Add bacon, broken into small pieces.
Cook over low heat, stirring constantly, until set.

Makes four sandwiches.

"In using old bacon much of the strong taste disappears if bacon is trimmed closely. Allow bacon to preboil for several minutes in water to which a teaspoon of baking soda has been added to a quart of water. Drain, rinse off and fry."

(Helpful Hint from the 1954 Region One Lookout Cookbook)

Beaver Ridge Ham Sandwich

Rolly (Sam) Grotte, 5 seasons
(1951-54 and 1995)
Bear Mountain LO, Hidden Peak LO,
Roundtop LO, Beaver Ridge LO
Clearwater National Forest
Idaho

Sam Grotte (second from left) back at Powell Ranger Station after being on lookout (1951)

butter

1 Tbsp. Worcestershire sauce (or soy sauce or teriyaki sauce)

1 slab of ham

Melt butter in fry pan and add about a tablespoon of Worcestershire sauce and fry a slab of ham. When you turn the ham, add another bit of Worcestershire sauce. That's it! It's great on a bagel. Try this recipe again, but replace the Worcestershire sauce with soy or teriyaki sauce.

"What Lookout has forgotten the days he's "closed up" for the season? For several days, heavy cloud cover (Cumulus Terminatus), rain and fog would blanket the tower. Cold, heavy winds would plaster the north and west windows with sheets of ice and snow. The phone would ring and the dispatcher would inform you it was time to close up.

Anxious to get back to civilization and warmer climes, you'd begin to chip ice from the hardware and windows so the shutters could be lowered and locked down. Food, official USFS cookware, and eating utensils would be stored. Finally, with the wood stove cold, you'd carefully climb onto the icy roof to cap the stovepipe. Like, as not, you'd shoulder a heavy pack, lock the door and the trapdoor to the catwalk and begin the hazardous slide down the excessively steep stairs. I say SLIDE because by this time there's so much of the white stuff you can't really find the stairs. It's time for the 10 mile hike to the trailhead and a hot shower." — Sam Grotte

Combination Sandwiches

From "The Lookout Cookbook, Region One" (1949)
submitted by Tom Slagle, 7 seasons (1960's)
(Dave Slagle's son, a second generation lookout)
Quartz Mountain Lookout
Colville National Forest
Washington

Tom Slagle's father Dave (on left) at Bodie Mountain LO in Washington with Tom's uncle Dick (1940's)

Mix together:

1/4 cup diced American cheese

1/2 tsp. dry mustard

2 Tbsp. cream

1/4 tsp. paprika

Cook and stir over boiling water until smooth. Cover and cook. Stir in 1/3 cup ground lunchmeat (frankfurters, wieners, bologna, canned lunchmeat or leftover cooked meat). Makes enough for 2 large sandwiches.

"While working as a forest fire lookout on Quartz Mountain in 1964, I was watching a small deer in the middle of the old road, about 300 feet from the tower. A cougar came out of the group of fir trees near the weather station and climbed out onto the rocks about 30 feet from the deer. It leaped at the deer! I had not realized that a deer could move so fast. They raced across the point of land to the southwest, and the deer was able to out-distance the cougar.

During those seven summers on Quartz, there were about 120 first sightings of fire for the Colville National Forest and the Indian Service. The mountain had an advantage as a lookout point. For, in addition to its 360 degrees of visibility, it was located in the middle of the valley, and would not be fogged in during electrical storms like the higher lookouts often were.

Now, when I come home to Republic, and drive over Sherman Pass, there are about 10 seconds when I can look up and see the top of Quartz Mountain. I always wonder if the tower will be there. It still is."

— Tom Slagle

French Fried Potatoes

From "The Lookout Cookbook, Region One" (1938)
submitted by Dick Slagle,
several seasons (1940's)
White Mountain LO, Columbia LO,
13 Mile LO, Sheep Mountain LO
Colville National Forest
Washington

Wash and pare potatoes. Cut into eighths lengthwise. Dry between towels and fry in deep fat. Drain on soft paper, sprinkle with salt and serve in an uncovered dish. The fat must not be too hot, as the potatoes must be cooked as well as browned.

Dick Slagle worked White Mountain Lookout in 1942 before going off to war for four years.

"My chief recollection of food during the summer of 1942 on White Mountain was that the cans of Campbell soup which we'd packed in at the beginning of the season proved to be not to my liking. The real gourmet dishes turned out to be potatoes and navy beans.

Immediately after that summer I was drafted into the army and so for four years during WWII I had the great memory of that pleasant time on the mountaintop. White Mountain was rather remote, three miles from the nearest forest road. My companion was a horse. There was a corral around the top of the mountain with a spring and the horse had a bell, which I could hear tinkling from time to time.

A band of sheep came through and I saw the herder once. Brother Dave came up for the weekend once and the ranger, Floyd Cory, came once. These were my visitors. Our communication was by phone, no radio. It was the usual one wire system with a ground wire and two phone batteries. The only other phone on the line was the local fish hatchery and they never used it. Twice a day the ranger station called, which meant that I didn't get to gab much with anyone else.

I guess the most exciting part was the lightning storms. Many times I would be awakened in the middle of the night by a soft ding of the telephone bell indicating that lightning had struck somewhere near the line. Then it would be a wait until the storm hit, then run out and throw the switch on the line, then huddle on the stool with glass insulators on the bottom until the storm passed."

— Dick Slagle

Breckenridge Lookout was built about 1931. It's an L-4 on a 40-foot tower and its viewing area includes 7 counties in California.

Breckenridge Chili Verde

Gordon Lindbery, 10 seasons
(1980's and 90's)
Breckenridge Lookout
Sequoia National Forest
California

4-6 lbs. fresh pork butt
26 oz. whole peeled tomatoes
1 medium onion, chopped
1-1/2 lbs. assorted chilies
1 28 oz. can Ortega brand Whole Green Chilies
6 tomatillos
1 bulb garlic
1/4 cup cilantro
2 fresh jalapeño peppers

Cut pork butt into toe-size pieces, trim fat. Mince garlic and saute in oil. Add pork and brown. Save juice. Scald fresh peppers and tomatillos, remove skin and seeds and coarsely chop. Roast jalapeños over flame, remove skin and seeds, and finely dice. Add coarsely chopped Ortega peppers and finely chopped cilantro. Combine ingredients and simmer about 3 hours with bone in pot. Remove excess fat.

Invite nearest engine crew to help eat and serve with flour tortillas.

"Great view, great folks, great fun—most of the time. For a late-in-life new career, this has been a richly rewarding experience."

— Gordon Lindbery

Orange-Oat Bars

(great trail food)

Chris Baker, 17 seasons (1988-2004)
Swiftcurrent LO, Huckleberry LO
Glacier National Park
Montana

Chris Baker at Swiftcurrent Lookout (2004)

Dough

1/2 cup brown sugar
1/4 cup white sugar
1 cup margarine
2 tsp. vanilla
1/2 tsp. salt
2 eggs
1 cup flour
1 cup rolled oats
1/2 cup chocolate chips

In a large bowl, beat thoroughly 1/2 cup brown sugar, margarine, vanilla, salt and eggs. Add the flour, rolled oats and chocolate chips and mix well. In a 9-inch greased pan, bake for 40 minutes at 350 degrees.

Syrup

3/4 cup white sugar
1/2 cup orange juice concentrate

In a saucepan, bring to a boil 1/4 cup white sugar and orange juice concentrate. Pour over hot cake. Cool and cut into bars.

Chewelah Mountain Lookout, Colville National Forest, Washington
By Tom Reul

Mrs. Hollis Stritch splits firewood for her stove in 1943 at West Fork Butte Lookout, Montana. (Photo by K.D. Swan)

Byam Deer Steaks with Brown Gravy

Larry Byam, 1 season (1997)
Coursey Lookout
Bienville National Forest
Mississippi

Forester Larry Byam (left) and archeologist Terry McClung (right) with the Coursey Lookout in the background (1997)

2 lbs. venison
3 cups bleached flour
2 heaping Tbsp. bleached flour
2 cups milk
1/2 tsp. salt
1 tsp. black pepper
1/2 tsp. garlic salt

Mix flour, salt, pepper and garlic salt together in a large container. Cut venison into strips about 1 inch wide and roll them in the flour mix. Slowly place each strip into a hot 12 inch skillet that contains about 1/4 to 1/2 inch of cooking oil. The oil should be hot enough that the steaks pop and sizzle when being placed in the skillet. Rotate once and remove when golden brown. As steaks are taken from the pan, more cooking oil may need to be added for the next pan full of floured steaks.

After cooking steaks, leave about 1/16 inch of the used cooking oil in the pan with all of the resulting crumbs that have fallen off the steaks while cooking (known locally as PAN DRIPPINGS). Stir in two heaping table-spoons of flour and stir. After the flour has soaked up all the grease and has turned brown, add 2 cups of milk and stir constantly.

When mixture comes to a rolling boil, reduce heat and simmer. Stir until mixture becomes thick. Add salt and pepper to taste. Deer steaks may be added to the gravy while in the pan or on the plate.

"Lightning storms will sneak up on you. You turn around and suddenly there they are, with lightning crashing down all around you. They tell you that the metal cab atop the metal tower is the safest place to be during a lightning storm, however, to stay in the tower feels contrary to your basic instincts for survival. You must fight the urge to run down and out of the tower. The experience is intensified as high winds buffet the 100-foot tower. It feels like the tower is swaying over two or three feet from side to side. You just know that it will buckle, snap, and throw you straight to the ground. It's a terrifying experience."

— Larry Byam

Note: Since 1990, Mississippi's 1.14 million acres of National Forest land have stopped using their lookouts for fire prevention, a function that has been replaced by aircraft. Today, some towers are used for mounting radio antennas, but most are slated for removal and will soon be sold as scrap. The prime reasons for removal involve concerns for public safety.

Vegetable Medley

Molly Morrison, 7 seasons (1970-73 & 1986-88)
Big Hole LO, Baldy Peak LO, Williams Peak LO
Lolo National Forest
Montana

Molly Morrison plays piano in the woodshed below Williams Peak Lookout in 1987. (Note the radio on the car hood!)

A closer view of Molly and her piano (1987)

2 Tbsp. olive oil
1/2 cup chopped onion (or dried)
2 cloves garlic, minced
1/2 tsp. salt
1/8 tsp. pepper
2 cups chopped mixed vegetables (carrots, zucchini, beans, etc.)
1/2 tsp. oregano
1/2 tsp. basil
2 cups water or stock
1 cup stewed tomatoes or tomato juice
3/4 cup cooked kidney or red beans
1/2 cup pasta
2 Tbsp. red wine (optional)
1/4 cup grated Parmesan cheese (optional)

> ***"The quiet of a mountaintop forces one to listen more carefully, observe more closely and to become in touch with one's thoughts."***
>
> ***— Molly Morrison***

Saute garlic and onion in olive oil until soft. Add salt, pepper, carrots (vegetables), oregano and basil. Cover and cook 5 minutes over high heat. Add stock, tomatoes, cooked beans and wine. Cover and simmer 15 minutes. Add pasta and simmer 10 or 15 more minutes. Top with grated Parmesan cheese. Serves 4-6.

Wyoming Jack Mulligan

Mark Schreiter, 17 seasons (1988-2004)
War Eagle LO, Pollock LO, Williams Peak,
Miner's LO,
Heaven's Gate LO, Pilot Peak LO
Payette National Forest
Idaho

Mark Schreiter at War Eagle Lookout (1996)

5 lbs. chicken
5 lbs. round steak
10 lbs. pork loin
2 bottles Worcestershire sauce
2 large cans stewed tomatoes
1 can carrots
1 can butter beans
6 Irish potatoes, finely chopped
1 lb. butter
1 can corn
1 can dark red kidney beans
1 large can mushrooms
6 onions, finely chopped
3 green peppers, finely chopped
2 red peppers
2 cloves garlic
1 can pimentos
1/2 bottle Tabasco sauce
1 bottle Kitchen Bouquet
1/2 pint olive oil
2 heaping Tbsp. mustard
1 bottle chili sauce
1/2 box paprika
6 lemons (juice)
salt and black pepper

"Wyoming Jack, (Mark Schreiter's illustrious great uncle), did everything in a big way, as this recipe attests. In honor of his memory, please don't even think of making any half batches!"

— Mark Schreiter

Finely chop chicken, round steak and pork loin and cook in a pot with one bottle of Worcestershire sauce. Cook stewed tomatoes, carrots, butter beans, Irish potatoes, butter, corn, kidney beans, mushrooms, onions, peppers and garlic until thoroughly done, then mix with meat in a large iron, copper or porcelain boiler. Add pimentos, Tabasco sauce, Kitchen Bouquet, olive oil, mustard, chili sauce, the other bottle of Worcestershire sauce, paprika, lemon juice and salt and pepper to taste. Cook Mulligan very slowly for at least two hours or until it becomes one uniform mass. Serve hot with hot garlic- buttered french bread and good beer.

Tobias Torrid-Tower Tort Chicken Tortilla Bake

Mary Ann Evans, 15 seasons (1990-2004)
Tobias Peak Lookout
Sequoia National Forest
California

Tobias Peak Lookout is located at 8,284 feet and was built in 1935.

"This is a cliffhanger!"

— Mary Ann Evans

3 cups shredded cooked chicken

2 cans (4 oz. each) chopped green chilies

1 cup chicken broth

1 can (10 3/4 oz.) cream of mushroom soup, undiluted

1 can (10 3/4 oz.) cream of chicken soup, undiluted

1 small onion, finely chopped

12 corn tortillas

2 cups (8 oz.) shredded cheddar cheese, divided

In a bowl combine chicken, chilies, broth, soups and onion. Warm tortillas. Layer half of tortillas on the bottom of a greased 13″x 9″ pan, cutting to fit pan if desired. Top with half of the chicken mix and cheese. Repeat layer. Bake uncovered at 350 degrees for 30 minutes.

Ms. Hawkins' Sweet Potato Casserole

Wydell Hawkins, 31 seasons (1937-1967)
Moore Tower
Bienville National Forest
Mississippi

Wydell Hawkins stands in front of the tower she worked from 1940 to 1967 in this photograph from the mid-1990's. Built in 1940, Moore Tower is Mississippi's tallest standing wooden structure and is the only fire tower built from wood left in the southeast.

3 cups sweet potatoes, cooked and mashed

1/2 cup sugar

1/2 cup milk

2 eggs, well-beaten

1/2 cup butter or margarine

1 Tbsp. vanilla

Topping:

1 cup brown sugar

1/2 cup flour

1/8 cup butter

1 cup pecans, chopped

Mix potatoes, sugar, eggs, milk, butter and vanilla. Place in buttered baking dish and set aside. Mix the brown sugar, flour, butter and pecans together and sprinkle on top of potato mixture. Bake in a 350 degree oven for about 25 minutes. Some may sprinkle a small amount of cinnamon over the top, but Ms. Hawkins prefers not to.

"We were proud of our jobs with the United States Forest Service. We had no televisions, AM-FM radios, magazines or books in our towers. We kept a constant vigilance on the horizon."

— Wydell Hawkins

Three Bean Salad

Pat Kneer, 17 seasons (1987-2004)
Pickett Peak LO, Hayfork Bally LO,
Limedyke LO, Ironside LO
Shasta-Trinity National Forest
California

1 can string beans

1 can garbanzo beans

1 can kidney beans

Drain beans. Add some chopped onions and/or garlic. Add anything else you like such as raw veggies, chicken or tofu. Then add any dressing you like.

48-foot high Hayfork Bally Lookout was built in 1972 and is located at 6363 feet. (1995)

"My most unforgettable time on a lookout was during the 1987 fires, our worst ever and my first year no less. Feeling an earthquake is quite unforgettable also.

I worked on the Hayfork Bally Lookout and several times the 48-foot tower shook, then swayed!! The hair stood up on my arms and my stomach felt queasy.

But my favorite is when the lightning storms come in...

I was born to be a fire lookout-ha! I love it." — Pat Kneer

Pat Kneer and friends looking southwest to the coast in 1994 from Ironside Lookout, which is located at 5350 feet and was built in the 1930's.

Shipwreck

From "The Lookout Cookbook, Region One" (1954)
Missoula, Montana

2 large onions

4 potatoes

4 stalks of celery or celery salt (optional)

1 lb. hamburger

1 can tomatoes

1 small can kidney beans

salt and pepper to taste

Into baking pan, put two layers of each of the following ingredients: raw, sliced potatoes, raw, sliced onions, chopped celery or sprinkle generously with celery salt, browned hamburger, and salt and pepper. Over this, pour tomatoes. Cover and cook 2 hours. Add kidney beans on top about 1/2 hour before serving.

This mobile lookout on top of Blizzard Peak on the Beaverhead National Forest, Montana was used in 1961 as a temporary lookout in areas where short-time fire hazards required continuous fire detection. The trailer also provided living facilities for small crews when not used as a lookout.

Virginia Vincent and Paleface at Stark Mountain Lookout, Montana (1989)

Radio-Traffic Ragout
(Takes no great concentration!)

Virginia H. Vincent, 35 seasons (1970-2004)
Red Hill Lookout
Wallowa-Whitman National Forest
Oregon
Stark Mountain Lookout
Lolo National Forest
Montana

diced boiled potato

canned tomatoes, well-drained (can have onion and green pepper mixed in)

canned corn, well-drained

diced tofu, flavored with basil pesto (pesto can be quite strong, so adjust to taste)

Heat first three ingredients over low heat so they don't stick in pan. Add tofu and continue to heat. Should not be runny. Leftovers can be added to soup, etc…

> ***"Green, brown, white, blue–***
>
> ***Lookout's summer view."***
>
> ***— Virginia H. Vincent***

Virginia Vincent plots the location of a fire using the alidade at Stark Mountain Lookout. (1989)

Thundering Posole

Karen Howell, 22 seasons (1983-2004)
Davenport LO, Grassy LO,
Mount Withington LO
Cibola National Forest
New Mexico

Karen Howell (left) at Davenport Lookout (1984)

1 onion, chopped

1 garlic bulb, chopped

1/2 tsp. black pepper

1/2 tsp. ground cumin

1/2 tsp. cayenne

1 1/2 lbs. pork shoulder (pre-stewed and cut into 1″ cubes)

3-5 cups broth from pork meat

2-3 cups pre-cooked posole or frozen or canned hominy

1 cup green chilies, diced

1 tsp. salt

optional ingredients:

crushed or powdered red chile

canned jalapeños

canned whole tomatoes

diced celery

"Posole is a stew made with hominy, pork and other ingredients which you can vary depending on what's available on your mountain. It's a favorite of mine for those chilly mountaintop days."

— Karen Howell

Saute onions and garlic in oil. Add the spices and stir. Stir in the pork, posole, broth, chilies and other ingredients. Cook at a simmer for 2-3 hours. Serve with tortillas, salsa and beans.

Baked Bean Hot Dish

Rod Schaefer, 27 seasons (1975-76,79,80,1982-2004)
Liscome Butte LO, Diamond Butte LO
Custer National Forest
Montana
Hogback LO, Sugarloaf LO
Shasta-Trinity National Forest
California

Sugarloaf Lookout with Mount Shasta in the distance (1994)

"Working on a lookout is like going on an extended camping trip while still enjoying all the comforts of home; a warm bed, a stocked cupboard, full kitchen facilities, hot and cold running lightning bolts, and a rattlesnake in the outhouse."

— Rod Schaefer

1 lb. lean hamburger
1 small diced onion
1/2 diced green pepper
3-4 sliced fresh mushrooms
1/2 cup brown or white sugar
2 16 oz. cans pork & beans
1 16 oz. can tomato sauce
1/3 cup ketchup
1 Tbsp. mustard
Worcestershire sauce to taste

Start browning hamburger; add the onion, green pepper and mushrooms and continue browning. Drain grease if desired. Add the rest of the ingredients and cook in a 350 degree oven for 45 minutes to an hour.

(On hot summer days, simmer on the stovetop; forget the oven.)

Serve with grated cheddar cheese and Doritos.

Pizza for 2 to 4

Sita Loveridge, 18 seasons
(1978, 1984-88, 1990, 1993-2001, 2003-2004)
Pilot Peak Lookout
Stanislaus National Forest
California
Hell's Half Acre LO, Lookout Mountain,
Willow Mountain LO, Deer Mountain LO
Bitterroot National Forest
Montana
Sheep Hill Lookout
Nez Perce National Forest
Idaho

Moon Shadow Loveridge at Sheep Hill Lookout, Idaho (1995)

"Lightning happens!"

— Sita Loveridge

1 tsp. honey
1 Tbsp. bread yeast
4 Tbsp. olive oil
3 cups whole wheat flour
1 14 oz. can crushed tomatoes, sauce or salsa
Italian spices (oregano, basil, parsley, etc…)
1 onion, thinly sliced
1 can olives, cut in half
1/2 to 1 can pineapple spears
mozzarella and Monterey Jack cheese, grated

Mix 1 cup warm water, honey and bread yeast in a large stainless steel or porcelain bowl. Let it sit until it's foamy. Add 1 tablespoon olive oil and up to 3 cups of whole wheat flour. Add flour until it just holds together and then shake flour over dough and knead it right in the bowl. Let sit in a warm place about 45 minutes. Spread 3 tablespoons olive oil into a 9"x 13" cake pan. Set raised dough in pan and flip over to get oil on top and bottom. Spread dough out to cover pan, forming a thicker crust around edges. Top with ingredients in the order they are listed. Bake in a 425 degree oven until the cheese bubbles. Let cool 5 minutes before eating.

East Spread Lookout was taken down on the Seeley Lake Ranger District in the 1970's.

Swimming Spam Blankets

Mark Sheets, 6 seasons
(1970-72, 1994, 2001, 2003)
East Spread Lookout
Pat's Knob (relief LO)
Eddy Mountain (relief LO)
Cougar Peak (relief LO)
Lolo National Forest
Montana

Mark Sheets, cooking at East Spread Lookout in 1971, was the last person to man the lookout in 1972.

1 can Spam

2 cups biscuit mix

1 Tbsp. butter

1/4 cup flour

1 to 2 cups milk (powdered okay)

Cut Spam into 6-8 long strips.

Mix biscuit mix according to directions. Roll out dough and cut into strips. Put strips of dough around Spam. Bake in a hot oven until biscuit dough is brown.

Melt butter in pan and stir in flour. Slowly add milk, stirring constantly until sauce is smooth. Simmer until done. Pour over biscuit-wrapped Spam. Bon Appetit!

> **"You learn how to live with yourself when you are the only person you see 24 hours a day."**
>
> **— Mark Sheets**

Chuck Wagon

Marie Green Hall, 29 seasons (1975-2004)
Iron Peak
California Dept of Forestry
Offield LO, Ukonom LO
Klamath National Forest
San Hedrin LO, Anthony Peak LO
Mendocino National Forest
California

Marie Green Hall at Anthony Peak LO (1994)

1 lb. ground chuck

1 large can baked beans

1 can green beans, drained

Brown ground chuck and add canned beans. Heat through. Add 1 tablespoon of brown sugar if desired. Makes 4 servings.

Marie Green Hall holds her daughter Lourance at Anthony Peak LO. (1986)

"I started in the mid-70's when I was told this is an obsolete job and I've been at it for 29 years now, and this is a job I love!"

— Marie Green Hall

Tamale Pie

Milicent Furrer, 5 seasons (1990's)
Anthony Peak (relief LO)
Mendocino National Forest
California

1 1/2 cups cold water
1 1/2 cups yellow cornmeal
1 1/2 tsp. salt
2 cups boiling water
1 lb. ground beef
1/2 cup chopped onion
1 Tbsp. flour
1 tsp. chili powder
1 can (1 lb.) tomatoes
1 can (8 oz.) whole kernel corn (drained)
1 can (4 oz.) Ortega brand Diced Green Chilies
1 can pitted black olives
shredded Jack or cheddar cheese

Combine and mix cold water and cornmeal. Add 1/2 tsp. salt to boiling water. Add cornmeal mixture, stirring constantly; bring to a boil. Partially cover pan and cook slowly for 7 minutes, stirring often. Line bottom and sides of a greased 2-quart casserole with cooked mush. Cook beef and onion in frying pan until beef is brown and crumbly. Stir in flour, remaining 1 tsp. salt and chili powder. Add tomatoes, breaking them up into chunks with a spoon. Stir in tomato sauce, corn, can of Ortega Diced Green Chilies and can of olives. Spoon into mush-lined casserole. Bake in 350 degree oven for about 35-40 minutes and then add cheese on top and return to oven for the last 5 minutes or so (until the cheese melts). Serve with fruit and green salad. Serves 6-8.

OPTIONAL: Cut this recipe in half to serve 4 and save the other half of the meat mixture for another meal by freezing or serve the following night over tortilla chips and a bed of lettuce with the meat mixture over the top of the lettuce. Top with sour cream and sprinkle with chopped green onions and slices of tomato on the side.

"Training days were warm with clear blue skies. It seemed obvious during my first storm that this was truly going to be "on the job training"...As cells bumped into cells, I was astonished at the sounds of the exploding thunder and the feeling of the power as it shook the huge timbers of the lookout itself. Thunder took on a new dimension in the midst of it instead of many miles from it. The lightning strikes were so close I began to pray to calm my fears. Then the cell phone rang and the ranger, knowing I was new to all this, called to check on me. He's laughing with excitement saying, "Isn't this great!!!" Yeah, you can say that because you're down there and not up here! If I get one more downstrike on Twin Rocks Ridge, I'm going out of service. O.K. Blah, blah, blah. Within 5 minutes I went out of service, sat on a wooden chair clutching my pillow with lightning strike sheet in hand wondering whatever possessed me to take a job with my office at 7,000 feet. I...who am afraid of heights!"

— Milicent Furrer

Anthony Peak Lookout was built in 1932 and then condemned twice, the first time in 1969. It was continually manned during remodeling in 1973, at which time it's now thought, the internal staircase was moved to the outside, and a new catwalk was installed.

The lookout was condemned the second time in 1990 as unsafe to occupy and the stairs were removed to prevent any entry. In 1993 the structure was extensively restored through the cooperative efforts of the USDA Forest Service and the Twin Rocks Landowners Association.

In 1994 Anthony Peak Lookout was reopened with a dedication ceremony and acknowledged as being registered in the National Historic Lookout Register and is once again manned as a fully operational Lookout.

Note: Marie Green Hall was instrumental (along with two others) in pushing for rehabilitation of the Anthony Peak Lookout after its closure in 1990.

Dolores Geffert-Decker at 8-Mile Tower (1972)

"Wonderful years, wonderful memories and still having contact with friends made during those years! Some of the best years of my life."

— Dolores Geffert-Decker

"Poached" Blue Grouse and Chicken Bake

Dolores Geffert-Decker, 16 seasons
(1964-65, 1967-80)
Glade Mountain LO, 8-Mile Tower
San Juan National Forest
Colorado

1 Blue Grouse (accidentally shot)

1 chicken (purchased)

potatoes, carrots, parsley, onion, celery, etc…

Place cleaned, whole birds in a roasting pan. Cut and clean veggies and place around birds. Season to taste. In a hot and working oven, bake at 350 degrees for 1 1/2 hours or until done.

8-Mile Tower from the air (1970)

Lookout Taters for Two

Helen McCrain, 2 seasons (1991-1992)
Summit Point Lookout
Wallowa-Whitman National Forest
Oregon

Summit Point Lookout (2002)

1 old iron skillet

3-4 medium spuds, diced

1 medium onion, chopped

vegetable oil

salt

sliced tomatoes

hot sauce

greens

Heat oil in skillet. Dump in spuds and onions. Cook until brown, turning often. Serve hot with sliced tomatoes, hot sauce, greens or whatever.

"Lookout Taters disappear fast!"

— Helen McCrain

Bear Mountain Mexicali Blues

Steve Kalling, 15 seasons (1990-2004)
Bear Mountain Lookout
Clearwater National Forest
Idaho

Steve Kalling at Bear Mountain Lookout (1996)

> ***"I don't get bored. I'm too curious. Everyday I go for water and everyday I study the amanita and contemplate my options."***
>
> ***— Steve Kalling***

1 can refried beans
1 jar salsa
1 cup cooked rice
1 onion, diced
3-5 corn tortillas
grated Romano cheese to taste
optional ingredients:
- *habañeros peppers*
- *fresh tomatoes*
- *cilantro*
- *veggies of any sort*

In a large, oiled cast iron skillet, layer tortillas, refried beans, onion, rice, cheese and salsa. Repeat several times ending with salsa and cheese.

Cover and bake in a preheated oven at 350 degrees for about 1 hour.

Serve with extra salsa and fresh spring water. (This recipe is great left over.)

Grizz's Road Kill Stew

Ray Kresek, 2 seasons (1955 & 1988)
Aeneas Lookout
Washington State Division of Forestry
Washington
Heaven's Gate Lookout
Wallowa-Whitman National Forest
Oregon

Ray Kresek working Heaven's Gate Lookout (1988)

1 cup chopped celery

3 medium-sized chopped carrots

3 spuds, quartered

6 wild onions (or 2 store-bought yellow ones, quartered)

4 cups water

1 lb. chopped elk sirloin (Can substitute with beef, a Rocky Mountain hen, or a porcupine, but be aware that this meat is very stringy and slightly piney in flavor. Could also use Bambi maybe.
Smokey Bear NEVER!)

"Once a lookout,

always a lookout".

— Ray Kresek

1/2 tsp. whole black pepper seeds

1 tsp. dried sage

1 tsp. salt

4 squirts Tabasco

1 fresh juniper twig (for ulcers)

1 fresh ceanothus "Buck Brush" leaf (for hemorrhoids)

2 Morel mushrooms, chopped fresh (when available)

Note: In a hurry? Pop open a can of Dinty Moore beef stew and eat 'til it's gone.

Bring it all to a boil on the C-S Official Lookout Stove if your wood's dry enough to get it that hot; then simmer with the lid on for 3 hours or more, or until well-seasoned and tender.

Chinese Chicken Wings

submitted by Joan Nelson Berrien
in memory of her mother,
Dorothy P. Nelson, 21 seasons (1961-81)
Hayfork Bally LO, Limedyke LO,
Plummer Peak LO
Shasta-Trinity National Forest
California

Plummer Peak Lookout where Dot spent most of her time as a lookout (1970's photo)

2 dozen chicken wings
1 tsp. sage
1 tsp. pepper
1/8 tsp. dry mustard
1/4 to 1/2 tsp. garlic powder
1 cup brown sugar
1/4 cup soy sauce
6 Tbsp. Worcestershire sauce

"Mom retired several years ago and passed away in 1989, but her good cooking was well-known."
— Joan Nelson Berrien

Prepare about 2 dozen chicken wings by cutting at the joints and discarding the tips. Combine the other ingredients in a saucepan and heat until the sugar is dissolved. Grease a 9"x 13" pan and put the chicken wings in it. Pour the sauce over the wings. Bake at 325-350 degrees for 1 hour stirring several times, covering the wings thoroughly with sauce.

Dot's son-in-law built this "Lookout Playhouse" in 1964 for her four grandsons when Dot was a lookout.

Dorothy P. Nelson at Plummer Peak Lookout (1970)

Advanced Lookout Training
Shasta-Trinity National Forest
Redding, California
June 4-5, 1968
Dorothy: second row, third from the left

Beef and Bean Stew

From "The Lookout Cookbook, Region One" (1954)
Missoula, Montana

4 slices diced bacon

1 lb. boneless stewing meat (or use a can of roast beef)

2 cups canned kidney or lima beans

1 cup canned tomatoes

1 onion, minced

celery salt (optional)

salt and pepper to taste

Fry bacon and add diced meat (brown first, if necessary), beans, tomatoes and seasoning. Place in buttered baking dish, cover and cook slowly about 2 hours. (If canned roast beef is used, cooking time may be reduced to one hour.)

Helen Merrick drew a sketch of a woodstove while working Jerry Johnson Lookout on the Clearwater National Forest, Idaho. (1952)

Dinner

WHAT'S COOKING ?

Helen Merrick's sketch of a bear visiting Jerry Johnson Lookout (1952)

White Clam Sauce and Linguini

Chris Baker, 17 seasons (1988-2004)
Swiftcurrent LO, Huckleberry LO
Glacier National Park
Montana

Huckleberry Lookout

"My lookout is 5 3/4 miles from the nearest road... All my supplies are packed in by mule train, and I find I can get most any ingredient up here if I'm just willing to box them correctly."

— Chris Baker

1/4 cup margarine
1/2 onion, chopped
1/2 tsp. garlic powder
2 Tbsp. flour
1 Tbsp. dry parsley flakes, if available
1 tsp. dry, powdered marjoram
1/2 tsp. salt
1/4 tsp. Tabasco, if available
3-10 1/2 oz. cans minced clams, drained with liquid saved

In a saucepan, melt margarine, and add onion and garlic. Cook three minutes. Sprinkle flour and stir, creating a roux. Add clam juice and heat. Add parsley, salt, marjoram and Tabasco. Slowly add more water or flour to either thin or thicken as desired. Add clams.

Cook linguini or spaghetti pasta in water with a dash of oil to avoid boil over. Serve clam sauce over pasta.

Chris Baker and her daughter Katie (photo on left) spent much of the summer together, along wtih Chris' two other children Daniel and David, at Huckleberry Lookout in 1994 while Chris' husband Bob was a backcountry ranger in Glacier National Park.

TTT Pot Pie

Donald Courtney, 7 seasons (1954, 1999-2004)
Cougar Peak LO,
Blue Mountain (relief LO)
Lolo National Forest
Montana

Don Courtney was the first lookout assigned to work the new Cougar Peak Lookout in 1954. He returned as a volunteer to help restore the lookout in 1995 through the Passport In Time program. Cougar Peak is now available for rent through the Forest Service lookout and cabin rental program.

1 can corned beef

any available vegetables (potatoes, green beans, carrots, peas, etc.)

pepper to taste

Bisquik dough

On top of stove, boil canned corned beef in enough water to make a consistent mush. Add all vegetables, chopped, and pepper to taste. When vegetables are approximately half cooked, drop Bisquik dough over the top and cover. Keep on low heat until dough is cooked.

"At the age of 19, we tend to know many things with certainty, but lack the confidence to make big moves without the authority of a printed label. We could gamble and we could experiment, but it was Bisquik that gave us the courage to start."

— Donald Courtney

Rod Schaefer at Sugarloaf Lookout with Mount Shasta in the background (1991)

Lookout Chili

Rod Schaefer, 27 seasons (1975-76,79,80,1982-2004)
Liscome Butte LO, Diamond Butte LO
Custer National Forest
Montana
Hogback LO, Sugarloaf LO
Shasta-Trinity National Forest
California

1 lb. lean hamburger or stew meat
1 small diced onion
Diced green pepper (to taste)
3-4 sliced fresh mushrooms
1 medium or large diced potato
1-16 oz. can kidney beans
1-16 oz. can tomato sauce
2 Tbsp. chili powder
1 tsp. oregano
3/4 tsp. onion salt
3/4 tsp. garlic salt
1/4 tsp. pepper
1 can whole tomatoes (optional)

Brown hamburger. Add the onion, green pepper and mushrooms and continue browning. Drain grease if desired and add the rest of the ingredients and simmer for 45 minutes to an hour until the diced potato is fully cooked.

Serve with grated cheddar cheese on top and use Doritos as a spoon.

"The countless hours of peace and solitude satisfy a need within me that carries over well into the off-season. It isn't just a job, it's a compulsion."

— Rod Schaefer

Mexi-Beef Casserole (stovetop)

Rita Kresek, 1 season (1988)
Heaven's Gate Lookout
Wallowa-Whitman National Forest
Oregon

Osborne Firefinder at Heaven's Gate Lookout

1 lb. ground beef
1 small onion, chopped
1-14 1/2 oz. can of tomatoes
1-16 oz. can kidney beans with liquid
1 small can green chilies
3/4 cup uncooked elbow macaroni
2 tsp. chili powder

In large skillet, crumble and brown beef and onion. Drain off fat. Add rest of ingredients and bring to a boil. Reduce heat to low and simmer gently (covered) about 20 minutes until macaroni is tender. Stir occasionally to prevent sticking.

"The sunrises and sunsets; starry nights and storm clouds; Northern lights and lightning... All these wonders are indelible forever in every lookout's memory."

— Rita Kresek

Tobin Kelly and Kristi Tranter at Union Peak Lookout, which is managed by the Montana Department of Natural Resources (1998)

> ***"Undoubtedly the worst cook in lookout history resided at Union Peak the summer of 1997. I wing it every time, not out of creativity, but from lack of skill. Life in a lookout is inherently a bit precarious and primitive in lifestyle. This recipe is too. If you try it, take similar safety precautions..."***
>
> ***— Kristi Tranter***

Italian Sub-Alpine Seafood Pasta

Kristi Tranter, 3 seasons (1997-1999)
Union Peak Lookout
Garnet Range
Montana

Pasta sauce (I look for the cheapest brand in a jar, then whichever "flavor" is lowest in fat.)

Pasta (Dry, bought in bulk to have a high energy stash of foodstuffs up there.)

Garlic (Fresh and lots of it. Hygiene is good, but nobody expects to find a beauty queen at a lookout with great breath.)

Herbs (Dry, Italian, basil, oregano, whatever, in bulk jars to liven things up at anytime.)

Tuna (From a can packed in water.)

Onion (One whole one chopped is a favorite way to go.)

Olive oil (Also bought in a bulk jar to have a ready stash. Use enough to keep the pot from scorching.)

Salt and pepper

Veggies optional (Steamed first if I'm willing to take the time, thrown in with the sauce if I'm not.)

Cook the pasta like the package says. In another saucepan, use a medium heat; stir around the olive oil and onion until the onion is sort of transparent. Crush or chop the garlic the way you like it and put that in with the onion. Take a couple of deep breaths, just for kicks. Pour in as much sauce as you fancy or to match the amount of pasta being cooked...a complete ensemble meal as a leftover is a good thing. Throw in herbs and pepper to please your delicate taste buds. With the herbs, I grab two finger-fulls myself, grind 'em up and sprinkle 'em in, like the real gourmets of my childhood did. The grand finale is to pour the now drained pasta into the saucepot and gently turn it all over and over to evenly distribute the sauce and noodles.

Elk Sausage Hash

Rowdy Ogden, 10 seasons (1991-2000)
Morrell Mountain Lookout
Lolo National Forest
Montana

elk sausage, spicy

potatoes

2 eggs

pepper

salt

canned ham, diced

Put elk in frying pan and cook until brown. Add potatoes and cook for about 5 minutes, until brown. Add ham. Cook for about 2 minutes until brown. Add eggs and cook until done. Add salt and pepper to taste.

Rowdy Ogden shared his lookout job with his dog Stag. (1994)

"Wear your snowshoes the first day of lookout season!"

— Rowdy Ogden

Rowdy's dog Wolbig at Morrell Mountain Lookout

Lightning Stir-Fry for One

Virginia Vincent, 35 seasons (1970-2004)
Red Hill Lookout
Wallowa-Whitman National Forest
Oregon
Stark Mountain Lookout
Lolo National Forest
Montana

1/2 cup sliced celery
1/2 cup sliced stem of bok choy (save and shred leaves)
or
1/2 cup cabbage, shredded
any amount of sliced onion or dried flakes
2-3 oz. firm tofu marinated in soy sauce flavored with powdered or fresh ginger root, a bit of honey, or brown sugar, dash of vinegar, garlic (powdered or fresh) and optional sherry or saki
1 Tbsp. oil
stir-fry or oyster sauce
3/4 cup chicken or beef broth (or bouillon)
1 Tbsp. cornstarch
optional: canned mushrooms
water chestnuts
bean sprouts

"Here I am alone
Exulting in sky above
And forest below."
— Virginia H. Vincent

Saute fresh vegetables in oil. Sprinkle with oyster sauce or stir-fry sauce and add chicken or beef broth/bouillon just enough to keep veggies moist. Add shredded bok choy leaves, cover and simmer until tender-crisp.

In 1/4 cup cold broth, dissolve cornstarch (if using 3/4 cup liquid). Stir into hot vegetables and broth, add tofu, and optional canned mushrooms, water chestnuts, bean sprouts, etc...

Cook stirring occasionally until liquid is transparent and thickened.

Serve on spaghetti, linguini, Chinese noodles, or 3/4 cup cooked rice.

Virginia Vincent visits her summer home, Stark Mountain Lookout, in Montana on March 31, 1974.

Bigas (Polish Dish)

Shirley Fellers, 6 seasons (1973-1978)
Hutch Mountain Lookout
Coconino National Forest
Arizona

Shirley Fellers (on left) and a visitor at Hutch Mountain Lookout (1973)

Hutch Mountain Fire LO, by Shirley Fellers

2 lbs. beef stew meat
2 lbs. lean pork
(4 lbs. ground meat can be substituted for above)
2 Tbsp. bacon drippings (or oil)
1 large onion, chopped
2 apples, chopped
1 medium cabbage, chopped
2 cups chopped tomatoes
1 can sauerkraut (washed)
1 tsp. sugar
1 bay leaf
salt and pepper
1 cup sherry (optional)

Brown meat in drippings or oil. Add rest of ingredients; simmer for 2- 2 1/2 hours or longer. This dish freezes well and is even better reheated.

Note: Girl Scouts in Poland sent this recipe to our Girl Scout troop in California in 1945 after we had sent cosmetic bags to them.

"Enjoyed doing a 5-year bird study - came in third for Conservationist of the Year for Arizona in 1978. Also, several hunters started using cameras instead of guns. Then they reported watching a mountain lion and two young playing east of the tower."

— Shirley Fellers

Spaghetti Sauce With Meatballs

Jack Fisher, 1 season (1956)
Camel's Hump Lookout
Kaniksu National Forest
Montana

Camel's Hump LO, Lolo National Forest (2004 photo by TJ Thomas)

Meatballs

1 1/2 lbs hamburger
1 large egg
1 tsp. cumin
salt and pepper to taste
1 cup cracker or bread crumbs
1 tsp. tarragon leaves
2 tsp. thyme

Mix all ingredients in large bowl, using your hands. (Don't overmix.) If mixture is too stiff, add skim milk or water. Form meatballs in your hands, 1" to 1 1/2" in diameter. Brown in a fry pan, but don't cook through. Or, bake at 425 degrees on baking sheets, sprayed with non-stick spray and bake for 12 minutes.

Sauce

1 qt. tomatoes
1 15-oz can tomato sauce
3 cloves garlic, smashed
1 tsp. sugar
1 tsp. thyme
1 or 2 6-oz cans tomato paste
1 lg onion chopped medium
fresh ground pepper—lots
1 1/2 tsp. oregano
2 bay leaves

Mix all ingredients in a deep sauce-pot; bring to a boil. Add meatballs and return to a boil; lower heat and simmer for about 1 hour. Cool to room temp and refrigerate or freeze for 2 to 3 days before using; this allows flavors to meld.

> ***"Camel's Hump was a tower with 50-foot legs. During one lightning storm the wind blew so strong the underside of the cab floor got wet. And with 2 inches of rot in each leg, things got a little nervous!" — Jack Fisher***

Survival Dinner

Ellen Hoeye Sedell, 1 season (1964)
Tom Rock Lookout
Department of Forestry
Oregon

Ellen Hoeye Sedell on the radio in 1964 at Tom Rock Lookout in Linn County, Oregon. Tom Rock was burned in 1978 in the "Lookout Reduction Program".

Slice of bread
(homemade in lookout woodstove)
Peanut Butter
(purchased prior to going up to lookout)
Homemade Jam
(from Mom)
Hard-boiled egg on the side,
sprinkled with salt and pepper
Ice Cream
(if the parents had visited that day)

"I was a 20-year-old college student. I didn't know how to cook and wasn't really interested in it; I did teach myself how to bake bread on the woodstove in the lookout. The ranger district staff told my parents they couldn't figure out what I was eating, since I never ordered anything for them to bring up. In retrospect I think I was practicing asceticism."

—Ellen Hoeye Sedell

Sliderock Slough

Liz (Peterson) Gupton, 1 season (1973)
Sliderock Lookout
Lolo National Forest
Montana

Sliderock Lookout was condemned in 1982 and was relocated to the Historical Museum at Fort Missoula in Montana.

1/2 cup butter or olive oil

1/2 cup fresh wild onions

1/2 lb of available meat (rabbit, grouse, venison; in-season of course!)

1/4 to 1/2 cup fresh cattail shoots

Get your pan sizzling hot with the butter or olive oil. Chop and sauté the fresh wild onions. (Note—do NOT confuse the wild onion with her slender counterpart, death camas!) When cooked, set aside (use a spatula to scoop them into a bowl, leaving the oil in the pan). Prepare (cube, slice, rip, tear) the meat and sauté/brown briefly in the hot oil. Then turn the heat down and cover. Simmer until meat is cooked. Stir in the fresh cattail shoots (plan on getting your feet wet when you gather them) and let them simmer/steam with the meat for 5-7 minutes. Oh, and don't forget the wild onions! They should go back in the pan with the cattails. Salt and pepper to taste and serve on rice (wild, of course!).

"My time on Sliderock was the formative educational experience that has helped me survive the last thirty-one years. If you can learn to live with yourself—solo—you've got a good start in life".

— Liz Gupton

Middle Sisters Lookout, St. Joe National Forest, Idaho
By Tom Reul

Emil Viche working Bear Gulch Lookout (1933)

Bear Gulch Lookout above Superior, Montana (1933)

Ernie Weber looking out from the crow's nest on Berray Mountain (1938)

> *"Ernie Weber's tales of his four summers on Berray, Green and Loveland lookouts on the old Cabinet NF led to his son Gary Weber's lifelong interest in lookouts, including his involvement in the Forest Fire Lookout Association and support of this book."*
>
> *— Gary A. Weber*

Lookout Special Chocolate Cake

submitted by Gary Weber
in memory of his father,
Ernie Weber, 4 seasons (1938-41)
Berray Mountain LO, Green Mountain LO,
Loveland Peak LO
Cabinet National Forest
Montana

2 cups sugar

3 cups flour

1 cup melted shortening

1/2 cup cold water

1 1/2 cups sour milk (can use sweet milk)

6 Tbsp. cocoa

2 eggs

2 tsp. soda

Mix all ingredients at once. Bake in a greased and floured pan at 350 degrees for 35-40 minutes in a 9"x13" pan.

Berray Mountain Lookout Cabin, Montana (1938)

Jinx's Make Do Raisin Tomato Pie

Arch & Jinx Archambeault, 1 season (1949)
Pilot Knob Lookout
Nez Perce National Forest
Idaho

Pilot Knob Lookout on the Nez Perce National Forest, Idaho (1949)

9-inch baked pie shell

1 cup raisins

1 shy cup water

1/2 cup sugar (preferably brown)

2 Tbsp. butter (if you have it)

1 or 2 Tbsp. cornstarch or flour for thickening

2 egg yolks (if you have them)

1/2 cup tomato juice

1/2 a tomato from canned tomatoes

(Who has lemon in the woods? This is the substitute.)

Heat raisins and water to boiling. Add sugar, butter and cornstarch or flour. Cook over low heat until thick. Remove from heat and add egg yolks, tomato juice and tomato. Cool the filling to the point that it will still pour. Fill the pie shell and cool. Top with meringue if desired. Cut and serve.

"The lookout was on 15 foot stilts and about 12 feet square. We had a grounded, single bed. Not a real hardship, though, because we were on our honeymoon. We were impressed that jello set in the spring and with snow on the 4th of July. This was probably a defining event for our marriage."

— Arch & Jinx Archambeault

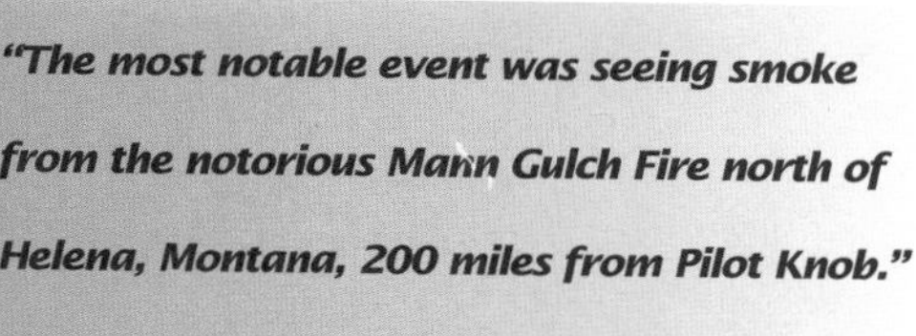

"The most notable event was seeing smoke from the notorious Mann Gulch Fire north of Helena, Montana, 200 miles from Pilot Knob."

— Arch & Jinx Archambeault

West Prospect Lookout is located at 8172 feet above sea level. (1999)

West Prospect Pistachio Salad

Wes Scarbrough, 1 season (1999)
West Prospect Lookout
Lassen National Forest
California

2-3 oz. packages of instant pistachio pudding
1 large container of Cool Whip
1 15 oz. can crushed pineapple
1 32 oz. container of cottage cheese
1/2 bag mini marshmallows

Mix all ingredients in a bowl and refrigerate.

"One of the most personally satisfying experiences of my life: to be a part of a team that protects a national park, two wilderness areas and a national forest from the ravages of wildfire."

— Wes Scarbrough

Wes Scarbrough at West Prospect LO (1999)

Huckleberry Buckle

Nancy, Erik and Ike Marks, 1 season (1987)
Gisborne Lookout
Idaho Panhandle National Forest
Idaho

Nancy Marks volunteered at Gisborne Lookout in the summer of 1987 along with her sons Erik and Ike and their dog and two cats.

1/2 cup shortening
1 1/4 cup sugar
1 egg
2 1/2 cups flour
2 1/2 tsp. baking powder
1/4 tsp. salt
1/2 cup milk
2 cups fresh huckleberries
1/2 tsp. cinnamon
1/4 cup margarine

Thoroughly cream shortening and 3/4 cup sugar; add egg and beat until light and fluffy.

Mix together 2 cups flour, baking powder and salt; add to creamed mixture alternately with milk.

Spread in greased 9"x13" pan. Top with berries.

Mix 1/2 cup sugar, 1/2 cup flour, and cinnamon; cut in butter until crumbly. Sprinkle over berries.

Bake at 350 degrees for 45 minutes. Cut into squares. Serve warm topped with whipped cream.

From Nancy's diary in August 1987 while on the lookout:

Weather: Sky- fogged in

Wind- south 15, gusts 25 (mod. Gusty)

Temp- dry 46, wet 46, relative humidity 100

Precip- .30 at 9am

I made two pies- a huckleberry pie and an apricot pie. I ran out of shortening so substituted margarine for half the shortening. Tasted great! Also didn't have a rolling pin so I put cold water in a Gatorade container and used it- worked first time. An interesting day for substitutions!"

— Nancy Marks

Red Devil Food Cake

From Myrl McKenna's 1933
Daily Log and Diary
Ninemile Lookout
Lolo National Forest
Montana

(Historical Museum at Fort Missoula –Kenneth C. McKenna collection)

Sketches done by Myrl McKenna who built and occupied the Ninemile Lookout in the early thirties

1 1/2 cups sifted flour
1/2 tsp. salt
1 cup sugar
2 eggs, well beaten
1/2 cup boiling water
1 tsp. baking powder
4 Tbsp. shortening or butter
1/2 cup sour milk
1/2 cup cocoa
1 tsp. vanilla

Sift flour once, add baking powder and salt and sift together three times. Cream butter thoroughly, add sugar gradually and cream until fluffy. Add eggs and beat after each addition until smooth. Add water to chocolate, mixing quickly. Add to cake batter and mix in vanilla. Mix thoroughly. Put in 2 buttered and floured 9" layer pans. Bake in oven set at 350 degrees for 25 minutes or until done.

"July 1929: (While building Bear Gulch LO)

30 Tuesday-8 hrs on tower.

Made one ladder for top of tower.

Put up banisters. Cut & cary (sic)

poles & bolted ladder and banisters.

(Dry Creek burning big)".

– Excerpt from Myrl McKenna's "IDEAS" book

"Cuppa" Cookies

Alice Wilkenson Allen
10 seasons (1940's and 50's)
Cougar Pass LO, Dean's Mountain LO,
Vaughn's Point LO, Trail Butte LO
Coos Forest Protective Association
Oregon

Alice Wilkenson Allen, Cougar Pass Lookout (1945)

1 cake mix, any flavor

1 cuppa oatmeal

1 cuppa chocolate chips

1 cuppa chopped nuts

1 cuppa raisins

1 cuppa anything else you can think of

Mix cake mix using 1/2 the liquid called for. Mix in remaining ingredients.

Drop, by the spoonful, on a greased cookie sheet. Bake about 15 minutes at 375 degrees, or until edges turn brown.

They're never the same, but always good.

"Lookouts were my ticket to college. I always looked forward to summer, and getting back to my 'castle in the sky'."

— Alice Wilkenson Allen

Bald Mountain Lookout, Oregon (1996)

Depression Fruit Cake

Sue A. Graham, 11 seasons
(1961-62, 1982-84, 1993-98)
Sugarloaf LO, King Mountain LO
Walker Mtn. LO, Spring Butte LO
Malheur National Forest
Bald Mountain LO
Fremont National Forest
Oregon

2 cups scalding water
2/3 cup shortening
1 cup cut-up dates
1 cup raisins
1/2 tsp. cloves
1/2 cup nut meats
1/2 pkg. citron fruit
1 tsp. cinnamon
1 tsp. nutmeg
1/2 tsp. salt

Mix and boil all ingredients in large pan for 8 minutes. Remove from heat, cool and add 4 cups flour and 2 teaspoons soda. Stir until smooth. Pour into greased loaf pans. Bake at 350 degrees for 45 minutes.

"Started with no days off, no refrigerator, and a wood cookstove to 5 days, 8 hours and all of the luxuries of home, (almost)."

— Sue A. Graham

Heavenly Huckleberry Happiness

Eugene Miller, 33 seasons
(1956-57, 1972-73, 1976-2004)
Blue Mountain Lookout, Priscilla Peak LO
Lolo National Forest
Montana

Eugene Miller and Tippy Toes on the catwalk at Blue Mountain Lookout (2004)

Filling

4 cups of huckleberries
1 1/2 cups sugar
4 Tbsp. flour
1/2 tsp. cinnamon
1/ 4 tsp. nutmeg
2 tsp. lemon juice
1 Tbsp. butter or margarine

Biscuit Mixture

1 cup flour
2 Tbsp. sugar
1 1/2 tsp. baking powder
1/4 tsp. salt
1 tsp. cinnamon
1/4 cup Crisco (butter flavored)
1 egg, slightly beaten
1/4 cup milk
1/2 tsp. vanilla

Combine filling ingredients and place in a large saucepan. Cook and stir on medium heat until mixture comes to a boil and thickens. Stir and simmer for one minute. Put into an 8" square or 2 quart baking dish. Place in oven at 375 degrees. Meanwhile, combine biscuit ingredients. It is best to combine flour, sugar, baking powder, salt and cinnamon, then cut into Crisco until crumbly. Combine slightly beaten egg with milk and vanilla. Add to flour mixture and stir until moistened. Drop biscuit mixture onto fruit in 8 mounds. Bake for 20 minutes or until golden brown. Serve warm with milk, cream, or ice cream if desired. Makes about 8 servings.

"This is where I gain back my sanity after a year of teaching school."

— Eugene Miller

"Smokejumper" Cake

Charlie and Bev Heebner, 15 seasons
(1959, 1990-98, 2000-04)
Sugarloaf Lookout
Wenatchee National Forest
Oregon Butte Lookout
Umatilla National Forest
Washington

Charlie Heebner worked Sugerloaf LO by himself in 1959.

1 cup brown sugar
1/2 cup margarine
2 1/4 cups flour
1 tsp. cinnamon
1 tsp. cloves
2 tsp. baking soda
1 pound canned applesauce
1 cup raisins
1 cup nuts

Cream margarine and sugar. Stir in dry ingredients alternately with applesauce. Fold in nuts and raisins. Put in greased 8 or 9 inch square pan. Bake at 350 degrees for about 40 minutes.

There is room for substitution here. I've used canned applesauce, sauce from dried apples, dates and many kinds of nuts. I do like raisins and walnuts the best.

> ***"Our motto on Oregon Butte: 'We find them, they fight them."***
>
> ***— Charlie & Bev Heebner***

Charlie and Bev Heebner have worked Oregon Butte LO together for 14 seasons. (1993)

Huckleberry-Apple Pie

Karla Padden, 5 seasons (1990's)
Richard's Peak Lookout
Lolo National Forest
Montana

Lisa and Rheanna Padden visit mom (Karla) at her lookout in 1994.

Pie crust

2 cups sifted all-purpose flour

1 tsp. salt

2/3 cup shortening

5-6 Tbsp. cold water

Sift flour and salt together. Cut in shortening, using a pastry blender or knife, until mixture is the size of small peas. Sprinkle water a little at a time over mixture stirring lightly with a fork until dough is just moist enough to hold together. Divide in half and form each into a ball. Roll out one ball on a floured surface and line a 9-inch pastry pan.

"When I'm at home, I use a crust recipe that has vinegar and eggs in it; but, on the lookout I never had all of those ingredients on hand, so I used this recipe".

— Karla Padden

Filling

2 cups huckleberries

3 large apples, peeled and sliced (preferably Red Delicious)

1 1/2 cups sugar

3/4 cup water

3-4 Tbsp. cornstarch (to thicken)

Combine all ingredients, except cornstarch, in a large pan. Heat until boiling. Dissolve cornstarch in 1/4 cup water, and slowly add to fruit mixture, stirring constantly. Pour filling into the 9-inch pastry pan. Roll out remaining dough. Moisten rim of bottom crust and place top crust over filling. Fold edge under bottom crust, pressing to seal. Flute edges and then cut slits in top crust for escape of steam. Bake at 375 degrees for 30-40 minutes or until golden brown.

Ziegler Mountain Lookout (1937)

Sweet Potato Pie

Pete Klinke, 5 seasons (1930's)
Ziegler Mountain Lookout
Kootenai National Forest
Montana

1 1/2 cups canned sweet potatoes, mashed
2 cups milk
2 eggs
1 tsp. cinnamon
1 Tbsp. butter
1 tsp. salt
2/3 cup sugar
1/2 tsp. lemon juice

Combine potatoes, milk, beaten egg yolks, cinnamon, butter, sugar and salt. Mix well. Fill a pastry-lined pie tin and cover with a lattice piecrust. Bake in hot oven about 25 minutes or until lattice is brown. Instead of lattice crust over pie, when cool, pie may be covered with meringue, browned lightly in oven and served hot.

"Probably the most memorable experience was the night a lightning storm came directly over the lookout. Blue flame was shooting about two feet from the telephone toward the stove. When the storm was over, I could hear a sizzling sound like bacon frying. Upon going outside to see if the roof was on fire, I found that every piece of metal on the outside of the cabin was covered by a blue glow and it looked as if a blue funnel was on top of the spark arrester. This is known as Saint Elmo's Fire."

— Pete Klinke

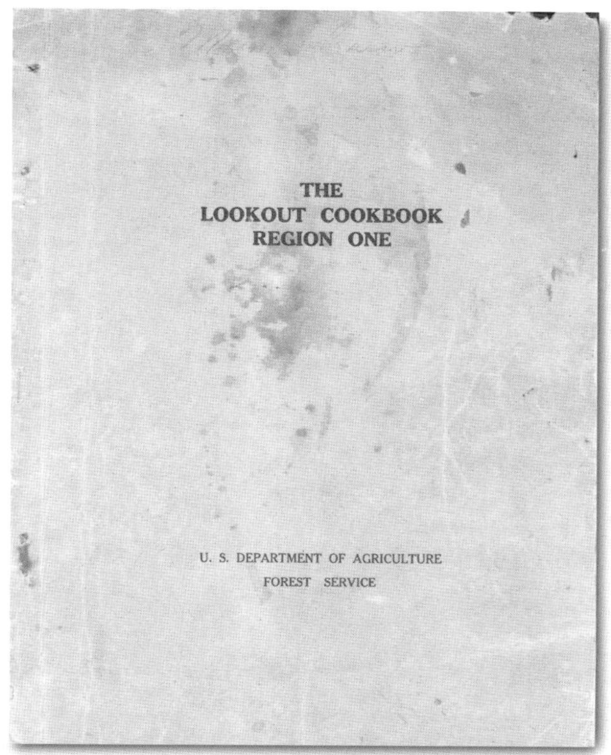

THE
LOOKOUT COOKBOOK
REGION ONE

U. S. DEPARTMENT OF AGRICULTURE
FOREST SERVICE

Cover of the 1938 Lookout Cookbook that was issued to lookouts by the Forest Service in Region One

"In 1937-1938 a lookout cookbook was printed on the Kootenai Forest. The recipes were submitted by the wives of Forest Service employees and called only for ingredients which were in the lookout rations. We paid 60 cents a day for meals while on a lookout, or 90 cents a day if we were where there was a cook... One interesting notation that I remember in our manual stated: "If only one man goes to a fire, he is the fire boss".

— Pete Klinke

THE LOOKOUT COOKBOOK INTRODUCTION

The idea of this book is to furnish tried and approved recipes in amounts suitable for one or two men which can be prepared from the food furnished the lookouts. The persons who furnished recipes were requested to refrain from calling for any food supplies not furnished. The book was tried out by nearly a hundred lookouts, smokechasers, small crews, etc., during the 1937 season and their comments and suggestions are included.

O.C. Bradeen,
Regional Supply Officer

Issued June 1, 1938

Introductory page of 1938 Lookout Cookbook

Rita and Ray's Alpine Huckleberry Pie

Rita and Ray Kresek, 1 season (1988)
Heaven's Gate Lookout
Wallowa-Whitman National Forest
Oregon

Ray Kresek, author of Fire Lookouts of the Northwest, standing in his backyard museum in Spokane, Washington (1997)

> ***"Rita's what keeps me going. She lets me drag home anything I want for the museum. But, she only lets me bring home one fire truck."***
>
> ***— Ray Kresek***

Filler

4 cups huckleberries (Picked fresh from the south slope at 8400 feet elevation.)

1 1/2 cups sugar

1/3 cup flour

1/2 tsp. cinnamon

1 1/2 Tbsp. margarine

Blend berries with the rest and dot margarine over berries.

Crust

2 cups flour

1/2 cup of Bruce Dreher's home rendered yearling bear grease (or 1 cup store-bought lard)

1/2 cup water

1/2 tsp. baking powder

Blend flour and grease. Add water and baking powder. Flatten into crust.

Pour 1 full sack of mesquite charcoal into the Comstock Castle official USFS Lookout Stove. (If you've ever tried to bake anything in this oven you'll know why you don't use wood from the regulation 14-day woodpile).

Bake 40-50 minutes at 400 degrees, if you can. Good luck.

Mountain Frosted Walnuts

Nancy R. Hood, 46 seasons, (1959-2004)
Dry Lake LO, Deadwood LO
Collins Baldy LO, Lake Mountain LO
Klamath National Forest
California

Nancy Hood (in uniform) gets a visit from E. Harris and Woody Clyburn at Collins Baldy Lookout in July 1978.

1 cup white sugar
1/3 tsp. cinnamon
1/3 cup canned milk
3/4 tsp. vanilla
2 cups walnut halves

Combine sugar, cinnamon, canned milk. Stir. Heat slowly to soft ball (234 degrees), stirring occasionally. Remove from heat. Add vanilla, then walnuts. Stir quickly until coated. Spread out on waxed paper to dry. Separate nuts. (Really nice to use walnut 1/2 pieces).

"I was born a hermit- I found my perfect job"!

— Nancy Hood

Chocolate Syrup

From "The Lookout Cookbook, Region One" (1938)
submitted by Dave Slagle, 3 seasons (1939-41)
Columbia Mountain LO, Fir Mountain LO
Colville National Forest
Washington

Fir Mountain Lookout, Washington (1940)

1/4 cup cocoa
1/8 tsp. salt
3/4 cup sugar
1/2 cup water
1/2 tsp. vanilla

Cook 5 to 7 minutes. Remove from heat. Add vanilla.
Store in a cold place.
Use 2 tablespoons to one cup of milk for cocoa.

"A warm summer spent on a lookout, with no visitors for many weeks, produces a state of euphoria, from which it is difficult to spring into quick action. Suddenly, there is a smoke, or a sheepherder looks you in the eye from about four feet, or an unexpected phone call will shake you up. It takes ten minutes to fill out a nervous fire report and quick action produces great excitement trying to get it called in before another lookout beats you to the phone. Was it really a fire? Or, was it dust from a band of sheep? Or, a wisp of fog? Or, a sawmill smoke coming up from the wrong ridge? How about a tail light, instead of a burning snag? I reported them all, usually with a "maybe". Most fires were easy to spot, the maybe's were tough on all of us, and sometimes humiliating. The firechasers had a tough time catching up with those tail lights."

— Dave Slagle

Boo Boo Berry Pie

Liz (Peterson) Gupton, 1 season (1973)
Sliderock Lookout
Lolo National Forest
Montana

3 cups of any combination of the following berries:
service berries, wild strawberries, whortleberries, huckleberries, black caps (like a wild blackberry), wild raspberries and rosehips (just the peels—no pithy centers)

3/4 cup of honey (can substitute 3/4 cup sugar for honey)
2 Tbsp. flour (or corn starch dissolved in water)
3 Tbsp. butter (melted)

Mix together and bake in a 9-inch pie shell at 350 degrees for 35 minutes.

Liz Gupton visits her old lookout at the Historical Museum at Fort Missoula. (2004)

"What a summer! I talked to ravens and coyotes, watched the most awe-inspiring sunsets, and got struck by lightning. (Fortunately, I was sitting in the captain's chair with the insulators on the legs). All experiences to last a lifetime!"

— Liz Gupton

Peachy Huckleberry Pie

Eugene Miller, 33 seasons
(1956-57, 1972-73, 1976-2004)
Blue Mountain LO, Priscilla Peak LO
Lolo National Forest
Montana

Gene gets a visit in 1999 from his wife, Myrtle, at Blue Mountain Lookout located above Missoula, Montana at 6460 feet.

Crust

2 cups flour

2/3 cup Crisco (butter flavored)

1/4 tsp. salt

1/8 cup cold water

Mix thoroughly flour, Crisco and salt until crumbly and no flour is seen separately. Add water and mix until a soft ball is formed. Take two pieces of wax paper about 14 inches long and put one of them on a flat surface. Take 2/3 of pastry ball and flatten it on the wax paper with your hands. Place second piece of wax paper over the dough and roll to 1/8" thickness, flipping dough over occasionally while rolling. Peel one piece of wax paper off at a sharp angle. Lay paper back on top and flip over. Peel second piece of wax paper off. Take rolled dough and flip onto a 9-inch pie plate (tin). Form dough to fit plate and trim off edges. Gather cut off pieces and mix with remaining dough and form the top crust the same way. Peel wax paper off both sides and cut small slits in center of crust. Lay wax paper over dough and set aside until ready to use.

Filling

1 peach- medium size

enough huckleberries to make 1 quart when added with peach

1 1/4 cups sugar

4 Tbsp. flour

1 tsp. cinnamon

1/4 tsp. nutmeg (optional)

1 large Tbsp. of butter (cut into small pieces)

Peel and slice peach into 1/8 to 1/4 inch thick pieces. Place in a measuring cup that holds one quart. Add huckleberries until fruit makes one quart together. In a two-cup measuring cup, combine sugar, flour, cinnamon and nutmeg and mix thoroughly. Then mix with fruit.

Put fruit mixture into piecrust. Place one large tablespoon of butter cut into small pieces on mixture. Moisten edges of crust with water until pasty. Place top crust on and trim to size. Use a fork and press the two crusts together. Bake in oven at 375 degrees for one hour.

"This is my penthouse in the sky."

— Eugene Miller

Sheep Mountain Lookout, Clearwater National Forest, Idaho
By Tom Reul

Miss Helen Dowe climbs the ladder to her lookout, Devil's Head Lookout Station, Pike National Forest, Colorado. (1919)

This Mountain Nourishes Me...

A Tribute to Beaver Ridge Lookout
Clearwater National Forest, Idaho
Inspired by my friend Nancy Allen Rose
A poem by
Chuck Petersen
1996

I am an intruder;
Families of eyes peer warily from the shadows.
Confusion, fear, concern give way to acceptance;
Not viewed as friend, but also not seen as enemy.
Not bothering, Not bothered.

Every voice is respected.
Racked bulls challenging, gathering autumn families.
Chirping grouse are harvesting grasshoppers, amongst
Scolding circus chipmunks who fall from highwire beargrass blooms.
Manic coyotes summon a smoke-cloaked moon;
All voices belong here.

Unaccustomed silence invades;
At first immense, becomes my friend.
Time to visit rooms of my mind, undusted for decades.
What was it that seemed so important all these years?
Straining at times to confirm I am still alive;
A droning horsefly draws me back.
Solitude fills my soul.

Each day is patiently vigilant, no need to rush.
Welcomed anticipation as the sun claws slowly to the ridge,
Spilling over shark's teeth to flood the veins.
Satisfied and reluctant, poised on the edge;
The sun bids farewell and is snapped from view;
Replaced by the stealth of night creatures.
Every hour, never to be seen again,
Afforded the same attention and respect.

Birth, Life, Death, relentless changes.
Some in minutes, others unseen;
The need to recycle is not questioned
Snow ghosts behind trees, williwaws claim more.
Rainless summer days; heating, drying, preparing.
A rumbling sky announces the start;
Releasing a hundred years of stored sunshine.
At times the cycle may yield to us;
Ultimately it will win and we must step aside.

I am a visitor; accepted, respected
Time to enjoy the Peace,
Peace to enjoy the Time.
This mountain nourishes me;
It tells me good stories.

Sentinels of Green Mountain

A poem by
Bruce Walker
Green Mountain Lookout, Oregon
1970-1974

Within these windows rest the all-seeing eyes of the high desert.
We are watchdogs for the juniper and sage in a range
Surrounded by hills and mountains to the north, the east,
the south, the west.

Our watchful eyes search for the first sign of smoke...
Signals which are translated to the presence of fire...
The age-old friend and enemy of Man;
Friendly when sponsored, but an enemy when unsupervised
And uncontrolled.

We may only sound the alarm by radio when smoke signs appear.
The fire crews assigned to the area respond to the location
Calculated and reported by the Lookout.
We do this not only because it is our job
But also because we love our beautiful and quiet
Oregon high desert land,

Not yet raped, spoiled, and polluted by over-population.
Fire, wild and unhampered, scorch the earth,
Destroy the grazing land, our homes, and above all
The wonders and beauty of our wonderful, wonderful Fort Rock
And Christmas Valley homeland.

Perhaps the unappreciative and unsympathetic eye sees not
The beauty in the gray sage, the green junipers,
The dark and golden rolling hills and the lava rock buttes.
But to those of us who live here by choice
In retirement, or wreak a living from its sand and rock.
We call it HOME.

The gnarled juniper, majestic in all its splendor, drilling its roots
Through sand and rock for life giving moisture, not only lends
Enchantment and beauty to the higher ground and sometimes the bare desert land,
But also provides shelter from the burning sun of summer and the
Cold driving winds of winter...shelter for the cattle and deer
And jacks and coyote and all the wild life which inhabit the area.
To all of them and to all of us who live here,
This is HOME.

We who stand by here at our Lookout as sentinels over all we survey,
Reporting fires as they occur, have a personal interest in our domain.
We hope and pray that as the years roll by we will be able
To look back with pride to our summers on our mountain and say,
"We did our best, the crews did the rest".
Yes, this is our country, our homeland, It is so beautiful,
Just as God made it. We have done our share to help keep it so...
We, the fire watch enjoined in a common cause
As the Sentinels of Green Mountain.

Myrle Walker fire watching from Green Mountain Lookout in 1971. Her husband Bruce and their dog Ebbie were with Myrle part of the time she was a lookout from 1970 to 1974.

Hutch Mountain Fire Lookout

A poem by
Shirley Fellers
Hutch Mountain Lookout, Arizona
1973-1978

Earthbound trees protest
wrestling with the gusty winds
tearing away leaves.

Tall lookout tower
perched upon a mountain top
guards the green Forest.

Wee, tiny cradle
hanging from a swaying branch
is vireo's nest.

Lightning strikes a tree,
blue smoke curls up and spreading
burns the dry forest.

Long hours in tower
ended with a rainy day
bringing quiet time.

Radio quiet,
no talk, no fires, everyone
is sleeping tonite.

New flying warblers
dart and catch a small insect
with good expertise.

Many good people
climb ev'ry steep tower step
to visit with us.

Fuzzy vireo
preening long on waving branch
oils his wing to fly.

Golden moon shining
between the dark thunderheads
promising clear skies.

In the still of night
aspens rustle in the wind
night birds are calling.

Summer sun setting
behind the Western mountains
makes soft velvet hues.

Deer in the meadow
question our intrusion
in their early rounds.

Elk bulls bugling
down the hill from the tower
while the young calves squeal.

Fog crept in early
to cover trees and flowers
and left diamonds.

Pockets of thin fog
arise from watering tanks
after a warm rain.

Solitaire flies high
strengthening wings and body
for a long flight south.

Long and lazy days
watching Aspen and Oak leaves
turn red and yellow.

THE MEN I MET I CAN'T FORGET, IT WAS EAST OF LOLO PASS
WHERE PINE AND SPRUCE SHELTER ELK AND MOOSE, AS
THEY WALK IN THE TALL BEAR GRASS. THERE'S ED McKAY
BIG BILL BELL, CHARLIE ALLEN AND JIM STILLWELL

THIS IS THE CELLWAY WHERE THE TALL PINE
GROW AND THE ROCKY PEAKS IS COVERED WITH SNOW
AND THE LOCKSAW RIVER RUNS SWIFT AND DEEP AND
THE RAINBOW TROUT SPOND, SWIM AND SLEEP.

THIS IS FIRE SEASON AND ALL IS LOCKED UP TIGHT
AND YOUR ON CALL BOTH DAY AND NIGHT. A SPOT
OF SMOKE IS ALWAYS BAD NEWS. YOU GRAB YOUR
HAT PACK AND SHOES AND YOU HEAD FOR THE BRUSH
AND YOU HARDLY KNOW WHERE BUT THE SMELL OF
SMOKE AND YOU KNOW YOUR THERE. YOU GRAB FOR
YOUR POLASKIE A FIRE FIGHTING TOOL AND DON'T
LEAVE THEM TILL THERE OUT IS A FORREST SERVICE
RULE.

THE DAYS ARE GROWING SHORTER AND THE NIGHTS
FROSTY AND COLD AND THE CEDER BEGIN TO SHED AND
THE TAMRACK TURNS GOLD. SO SOON I'LL BE LEAVING
THESE PEAKS WITH THE BIG SNOW CONES AND HEAD
DOWN THAT TRAIL THAT HEADS FOR HOME

MYRL McKENNA 1933

A poem by Myrl McKenna, Ninemile LO & Bear Gulch LO, Montana (1929-1933)

Copper Mountain Lookout, Coeur D'Alene National Forest, Idaho
By Tom Reul

A Brief History of Lookouts

Jodi Allison-Bunnell
Archivist
Missoula, Montana

Lookout towers were created for a purely utilitarian reason: to aid in fire prevention and control in forests. The United States Forest Service was created from the Bureau of Forestry within the Department of Agriculture in 1905. With Gifford Pinchot's appointment as first head of the Forest Service, the new agency worked to preserve and promote the economic utility of forests. Trees burned meant money lost; the agency immediately began some work on fire control.

In 1910, the worst forest fires in the twentieth century burned about five million acres in the national forests, three million of those in timber-rich Idaho and Montana, and killed seventy-eight fire fighters. This seemingly all-out attack of nature on man's economic interests pushed the Forest Service to begin a decade of rigorous investigation of a fire protection system. Their goal: total eradication of destructive fire in the forests. Fires had to be detected while they were still small and easy to control; waiting until the smoke reached a populated area was waiting too long. This meant stationing people in remote areas to watch for plumes of smoke.

Ranger on fire patrol duty in Montana (1909)

A Brief History of Lookouts

In 1911, William Bushnell Osborne of Portland, Oregon, invented the firefinder that has since been used in most lookout towers in the United States: a circular map with a brass alidade mounted on it, oriented to the surrounding landscape. The first fire lookouts perched a firefinder on a high peak or scaled a tall tree and built a "crow's nest" on top of it. They lived in canvas tents with little or no protection from the elements, including lightning. The first permanent lookouts, including cabins with lookout cupolas and the first tall towers, were constructed starting in the 1910s. A fairly standard tower design, with a 14-by-14 or 12-by-12-foot glass-walled, hip-roofed house on wooden legs 14 to 90 feet high, kept stable by heavy guy wires that connected to a lightning rod at the peak of the roof. Shutters shaded the windows, and an Osborne firefinder was mounted on a post in the center of the lookout. Communication was by heliograph, then by miles of telephone wire, then by radio. Lookouts had systematic regimens for looking for smokes, as prescribed by Osborne's 1924 Western Fire Fighter's Manual. Strict regulations, including systematic eye tests and detailed lists of chores, were enforced by surprise inspections.

With a series of spectacular fires in the early 1930s, including the Matilija (1932) in California, the Tillamook (1933) in Oregon, and the Selway fires (1934) in the northern Rocky Mountains, federal fire protection became an even higher priority. Between April 5, 1933, and June 30, 1942, the Civilian Conservation Corps constructed 1,187 lookout houses and 3,116 lookout towers as part of its massive fire protection program.

Indian Grave Lookout Construction in 1934, Clearwater National Forest Idaho (Viche Family photo collection)

By 1953, there were 5,060 permanent lookout stations built in the national forests, mostly in the heavily forested states of Washington (646 stations), Oregon (805 stations), Idaho (966 stations) and Montana (626 stations). While these lookouts were never all in simultaneous use, the early systems did rely primarily on lookouts being stationed relatively close together with intersecting sight lines.

Little Guard Lookout on the Coeur d'Alene National Forest (1959)

Lookouts and the towers quickly became central images in the Forest Services educational campaigns aimed at raising public awareness of fire and at managing behavior. A lookout on Oregon's Mount Hood appeared in a Forest Service film, *Red Enemy*, in the 1910s heroically calling out a fire crew to protect forests, "God's first temple." Lookouts appear constantly in forest recreation guides from the 1930s to the 1950s; captions under pictures of leggy towers and lookouts peering through binoculars remind the reader that the lookout is ever-vigilant and is even keeping an eye on your activities. Forest visitors were encouraged to visit the lookout towers and to find out how fires were located and extinguished, so that they would be more careful with fire themselves. Towers became automobile trip destinations for the striking views of the surrounding forest.

But the glory days of the lookouts were fleeting. Lookouts were augmented with air patrols as early as 1915. Air patrols increased after World War II, as surplus war equipment was used for fire control. By the 1950s, networks of roads built in the forests and smokejumpers dropped from airplanes meant that fire were more quickly reached. Speed of detection was no longer as crucial, and towers were slowly abandoned. In 1965, the Forest Service, concerned that persons injured exploring or climbing on abandoned lookouts would file lawsuits, ordered abandoned towers dismantled or burned. Many were lost forever.

The Forest Service destroyed many abandoned lookouts, starting in the 1960's. (Viche Family collection)

But many that remain are finding a new life as summer cabins or shelters for hikers and climbers. Some have been moved to ranger stations or museums for use as interpretive centers.

In face of many years of research into fire and forest ecology, the Forest Service has changed its policy; some fires are left to burn for their positive effects on the forest. Fire has a place in the forest once again, no longer a "red enemy," but a paradoxical friend. The fire lookouts are a symbol of a perception of nature and science in this century that will persist in the national imagination.

Types of Lookouts

Gary Weber
FFLA, Montana / N. Idaho Chapter Director

The early years of fixed detection saw ingenuity at its best from local foresters. A perch on a large branch of a broken-off tree was one of the first "lookouts" in the west. Crow's nest perches were established in the tops of the tallest trees, makeshift towers elevated observers above their surroundings, and on open mountaintops, maps set atop short posts or at ground level served the purpose. Canvas tent living quarters were a luxury at many of these sites.

Crow's Nest
Montana
(Gary Weber's collection)

The first "standard" U.S. Forest Service design was Lige Coalman's D-6 cupola placed atop Mount Hood, Oregon's highest point, in 1915. The 12′ x 12′ hip-roofed frame house had windows all around, with a quarter size glassed-in second story to serve as its observatory. Nearly two hundred eventually made it to the high points of Oregon, Washington, Idaho and Montana. "D-6" referred to District 6 of the USFS, Oregon and Washington, now called Region 6.

D-6 Cupola
(Viche Family collection)

Types of Lookouts

In 1922 D. L. Beatty's first D-1 cupola house appeared atop Hornet Peak on the Flathead National Forest in Montana. This 14' x 14' gable-roofed log cabin, complete with framed glass cupola was followed by several similar designs. The Nez Perce Forest's "R-3" had hand-hewn dovetail-tenon notched corners and was truly a mark of fine craftsmen. Later, standard plans in Region One included L-2 frame and L-3 log gable-roofed cupola lookout houses. Other "non-standard" cupola lookout houses were abundant.

D-1 Cupola (Viche Family collection)

In 1929, the prototypes appeared for the next generation of lookout houses. The L-4 model, with its 14' x 14' frame cab cost only $500 (FOB Spokane or Portland); was bundled in kits for hauling by mule trains; and would even fit atop pole towers. The earliest L-4's had a gable roof, with heavy window shutters providing shade, held horizontal above the windows by 2" x 2" struts.

1930 L-4 (Viche Family collection)

The 1933 L-4 model had a hip roof instead of the gable roof. Region Six's 1936 L-4 design maintained the hip roof, but featured bolts from extended ceiling joists to hold the shutters open. They're often referred to as Aladdins, named for their principal manufacturer. More than a thousand L-4 houses were placed on the rocks, above cinder block or log crib basements, or atop towers ranging from 10 to 84 feet. The earlier towers were constructed from poles cut on-site, while the later ones were placed atop creosote-treated timber towers. Over a half-century after the last L-4 was built, a few hundred are standing, with many still in service. Similar designs received other names elsewhere across the west.

1933 L-4
Jerry Johnson L.O., Idaho
(Viche Family collection)

Types of Lookouts

The L-4 had its "little brothers", the L-5 and the L-6. Region Six's L-5 was a 10' x 10' version of the L-4, placed primarily at secondary patrol points, but only a few were lived in. (To confuse matters, Region One's "L-5" was a log version of the 1929 gable-roof L-4.)

L-5
Skookum Butte Lookout
Idaho / Montana line
(2004)

The L-6 measured 8' x 8', and frequently found itself atop 80 to 100 foot wooden towers, although a few were built on the ground or on low log cribbings. The L-6 was primarily used as a secondary patrol lookout, although some served on primary points with ground living quarters.

L-6
Old Horseshoe Lookout
(Viche Family collection)

In 1953, the flat-roofed tarpaper and plywood "R-6 Flat" became the latest and greatest lookout design. This wooden design lasted until the 1990's when other designs were constructed, including an 8-sided octagonal cab, and a modified version of the original gable-roofed L-4.

R-6
Yaak Mountain, Montana

L-4 (next to steel tower)
Warland Peak, Montana

While wooden lookout structures were the norm in the northwest, the most common lookout structure nationwide was the galvanized steel tower with a 7' x 7' cab. While many of these rose a hundred feet above ground, one still tops out 175 feet in the air! Aermotor (well known for their windmills) was the principal provider of these towers, although other manufacturers' names included International Derrick, Blaw-Knox, Pacific Coast Steel and McClintock-Marshall.

While Aermotor manufactured a few "live-in" cab models, the modern steel equivalent to the R-6 Flat is the CL-100 series. These steel towers and houses with their flat corrugated steel roofs are most frequently found in California and the southwest.

The Osborne Firefinder

Mr. and Mrs. Merrill Edmunds using the Osborne Firefinder at Antrim Point Lookout in July 1943. They had been married only a short time and spent their honeymoon at the lookout on the Lolo National Forest, Montana.

The Osborne Firefinder

The Osborne Firefinder is the most widely used fire plotting instrument in the world. It was originally created in 1911 by W. B. Osborne, a forester for the USDA Forest Service. Osborne modified his original design several times throughout the years until 1934 when he created the instrument design that is still used today.

A volunteer with the Angeles National Forest wrote of her experience using the Osborne Firefinder in the October 1996 Angeles Volunteer News:

> ***"When I was first introduced to the Osborne Firefinder, I was amazed how easy it was to pinpoint the area where I had observed some smoke. Just line up the horsehair in the front sight (similar to a rifle sight) with the base of the fire and the peephole in the rear sight. Once the hair is properly aligned with the smoke, take the horizontal reading in degrees and minutes. Then obtain the vertical angle reading by using the measurement on the sliding metal piece on the rear sight and estimate the miles between the tower and the sight of the smoke using the metal tape on the Osborne Firefinder. After checking the map which is calibrated to my tower's location and affixed to the Firefinder, I can pinpoint the area of a fire very closely."***
>
> ***— Angeles National Forest Volunteer***

Blue Mountain Lookout, Kootenai National Forest, Montana
By Tom Reul

Get Involved

Forest Fire Lookout Association

The Forest Fire Lookout Association (FFLA), founded in 1990, is an organization involved in research and promoting public awareness of current and former forest fire lookout sites, ground cabins, and early forest fire detection methods.

Lookout and Smokechaser at Jackknife Lookout in North Idaho (circa 1932)

The organization also helps facilitate restoration of threatened lookouts by cooperating with federal, state, and private landowners along with private and public groups.

Here are some examples of how you can help:

- Join the FFLA.
- Volunteer to participate in a lookout restoration project.
- Make a tax-deductible financial contribution (FFLA is a 501(c)3 organization).
- Travel to lookout sites and participate in preparing nominations to the National Historic Lookout Register.

For more information on how you can help, go to www.firelookout.org

Montana's Little Joe Lookout in 1946 (Frances Hamilton photo)

Passport in Time

A Volunteer Program
of the
USDA Forest Service

Passport In Time (PIT) is a volunteer Forest Service program that invites the public to participate in historic preservation projects on national forests across the country. You may choose among activities such as restoring lookouts and other buildings, archaeological excavation, survey, site mapping, collecting oral histories, and archival research.

Lookout Tree and 1906 fireman's cabin on Sliderock Mountain, Montana (circa 1910)

The projects vary in length, but most are one week long. There is no registration fee. Facilities vary depending on the activity and location. Many projects involve backcountry camping where volunteers are responsible for their own food and gear. Others offer meals prepared by a "camp cook". Still others provide hook-ups for RV's, or volunteers may stay at local hotels.

PIT Volunteers restore the 1906 fireman's cabin on Sliderock Mountain, July 1998.

Passport in Time

The "PIT Traveler," a free newsletter announcing current projects and containing an application, is published twice a year in March and September. To receive the "PIT Traveler," contact the Passport In Time Clearinghouse. Or you can check the website for the same project listings and the application form. The USDA is an equal opportunity provider and employer.

Passport In Time Clearinghouse
PO Box 31315
Tucson, AZ 85751-1315
1-800-281-9176 (24 hours, Voice/TTY)
520-722-2716 (Tucson)
pit@sricrm.com
www.passportintime.com

Kathy Johnson helped restore the Sliderock Fireman's cabin in 1998.

Emily Langston visits the restored West Fork Butte Lookout while volunteering with Joyce Garrett as chefs for the restoration project on Sliderock Mountain in 1998. Both lookouts are on the Lolo National Forest in Montana.

Volunteer
Be a Lookout

Spotted Bear Lookout in the Flathead-Swan River Region, Montana (1923)

Contact the Forest Service office of your choice to see if you can volunteer to be a lookout for a season. Limited opportunities are available.

Rent a Lookout

Cindy Holder rented Arid Peak Lookout on the Idaho Panhandle National Forest in 2002, a few years after members of the FFLA restored it.

To rent a lookout:

- Call the Forest Service
- Visit the Forest Service websites
- Go to www.firelookout.net

Many national forests rent lookouts. (Shaded states offer lookouts for rent).

Spy Glass Peak Lookout, Coeur d'Alene National Forest, Idaho
By Tom Reul

NATIONAL HISTORIC PRESERVATION ACT OF 1966:
(last amended in 1992)

Section 106:

"The head of any Federal agency having...jurisdiction over a(n)...undertaking...shall...take into account the effect of the undertaking on any...site, building, structure, or object that is included in or eligible for inclusion in the National Register..."

Section 110 (16 U.S.C. 470h-2):

(a)(1) "The heads of all Federal agencies shall assume responsibility for the preservation of historic properties which are owned or controlled by such agency..."

(2) "...each Federal agency shall establish a program to locate, inventory, and nominate to the secretary all properties under the agency's ownership...that appear to qualify for inclusion on the National Register... Each Federal agency shall exercise caution to assure that any such property...is not inadvertently transferred, sold, demolished, substantially altered, or allowed to deteriorate significantly..."

ANTIQUITIES ACT OF 1906:

"...any person who shall...injure or destroy any historic...ruin or monument...situated on lands owned...by the Government...shall be fined...and/or imprisoned".

ARCHAEOLOGICAL RESOURCES PROTECTION ACT OF 1979:
(last amended in 1988)

"...The purpose of this Act...is to secure...the protection of archaeological resources and sites which are on public lands..."

Junction Mountain Lookout, Clearwater National Forest, Idaho By Tom Reul

LEAVE NO TRACE
OUTDOOR ETHICS

Plan Ahead And Prepare

Know area regulations and concerns, keep party size small (2-6), pack proper equipment like map, compass and water filter. Repackage food into plastic bags.

Travel And Camp On Durable Surfaces

On the Trail: Use existing trails, stay on switchbacks, travel cross-country on rock, gravel, dry grasses or snow. Step to downhill side of trail and speak softly when encountering livestock.

At Camp: Use existing sites that are 200 feet (70 adult steps) from water to keep water clean, to allow animals to drink and to protect vegetation. Wear soft-soled shoes to lessen soil compaction.

Dispose Of Waste Properly

Place human waste in catholes (4"-6" deep) 200 feet from water, camp and trail. Pack out toilet paper or bury with waste. Wash yourself and dishes with biodegradable soap 200 feet from water. Scatter strained dish water. Pack out strained food.

Leave What You Find

Respect your natural heritage by leaving plants, rocks and historic artifacts as you find them. Good campsites are found, not made. Altering sites by building structures or trenches is not necessary when you have proper equipment and camping skills.

Minimize Campfire Impacts

Camp stoves minimize impacts to the backcountry. Enjoy a candle lantern instead of a fire. Where campfires are permitted, use an existing fire ring, or bring a fire pan to avoid creating more scars. Gather wrist-sized sticks from the ground, not from live trees.

Make sure your campfire is out by placing hand in cooled ashes. Remove and pack out unburned trash from campfire and scatter cooled ashes far from camp, trail and water.

Respect Wildlife

Observe from a distance. Avoid sensitive times and habitats. Control your pet. Never feed wild animals. Store food and trash securely. Hang food from tree limbs 12 feet off the ground, 6 feet from the tree‘s trunk and 6 feet below the supporting limb.

Be Considerate Of Other Visitors

Respect other visitors. Yield to others. Keep a low profile. Let nature‘s sounds prevail.

Spotted Bear Lookout, Flathead National Forest, Montana
By Tom Reul

Lookout Bibliography

Jodi Allison-Bunnell

I compiled the following bibliography in June 2004, based on searches of OCLC (Online Computer Library Center) and the National Union Catalog of Manuscript Collections. I also used others' bibliographies and my research files. I include full-length books, archival resources, and websites about lookouts in the United States. The subject terms used in library catalogs that are most relevant to fire lookouts are Fire Lookouts and Fire Lookout Stations. Information about lookouts can also be found under more general subjects, including Forest Fires–Prevention and Control.

Entries are divided into eleven categories: Archives and Records, Biography and Personal Narratives, Cookbooks, Juvenile Fiction, Fiction and Poetry, History, Historic Preservation, Historic Works, Oral Histories, Travel Guides, and Websites. Within each category, entries are arranged alphabetically.

Archives and Records

The National Archives in Washington DC has considerable records, photographs, and moving images relating to fire lookouts in the records of the United States Forest Service (Record Group 95), National Park Service (Record Group 79), and the Bureau of Land Management. Regional offices in Seattle, Denver, and Laguna Niguel and San Bruno, California also have substantial collections relating to fire lookouts on federal lands in the West. Some national parks have park archives with records on fire management, lookout diaries, and photographs. Records on lookouts at state archives are most likely to be found in the records of the state fire management or forestry division.

There are also a few personal archival collections from lookouts. Search the National Union Catalog of Manuscript Collections at http://www.loc.gov/coll/nucmc/nucmc.html to find them.

Biography and Personal Narratives

Abbey, Edward. *Freedom and Wilderness* (sound recording). Audio Press, 1987.

Beatty, Jeanne. *Lookout Wife.* New York: Random House, 1953.

Bill, Joe. *Climbing the Ladder Less Traveled: Adventures, Insights and Life Journeys.* Fountainhills, Ariz.: Mountain Forest Pub., 2002.

Binning, Esther L. *The Summer of 1920 on Smith Mountain Fire Lookout, Weiser National Forest, Idaho.* [McCall, Idaho?]: Heritage Program, Payette National Forest, USDA, Intermountain Region, 2000.

Calahan, David. *Snow Camp Lookout: View with a Room, Mouse Included.* Medford, Or.: In-Forms Pub., 1996.

Carlson, Vada F., and Fred Turley. *Fred Turley and Promontory Lookout.* Winslow, AZ.: D.R. Ayres, 1987.

Chriswell, Harold C. *Memoirs: Harold C. (Chris) Chriswell, 1933 to 1971.* [Wash.?] : U.S. Forest Service, Dept. of Agriculture, 1989.

Coffman, Harold E. *This is our Forest: a Collection of Stories from a Lookout Smokechaser who Worked in the Bitterroot Mountains of Montana and Idaho.* Sun City, Arizona: HalMar Publications, 2000.

Ellingson, John. *Fire Lookout: a College Boy's Summer in 1941.* Spokane, Wash.: Westerners, Spokane Corral, 2001.

Hardy, Martha. *Tatoosh.* New York: Macmillan, 1946. (Reissued by the Mountaineers, 1980)

Higman, Harry and Earl Larrison. *Pilchuck: The Life of a Mountain.* Superior Publishing, 1949.

Johnson, Alice. *Walls of Glass on a Mountaintop: My Six Years as a Fire Lookout.* Laramie, Wy.: Jelm Mountain Publications, 1989.

Maughan, Jackie Johnson. *Go Tell It on the Mountain.* Mechanicsburg, PA: Stackpole Books, 1996.

Seaman, Frances Boone. *Nehasane Fire Observer: an Adirondack Woman's Summer of '42.* Utica, N.Y.: Nicholas K. Burns Pub., 2002.

Scheese, Don. *Mountains of Memory: a Fire Lookout's Life in the River of No Return Wilderness.* Iowa City: University of Iowa Press, 2001.

Yahr, Warren. *Smokechaser.* Moscow, ID: University of Idaho Press, 1995.

Cookbooks

United States. Forest Service. Northern Region. *The lookout cookbook: region one. [S.1.:s.n., 1938.] (Reissued 1954, 1966)*

United States. Forest Service. Northern Region. *The lookout cookbook: region one. [S.1.:s.n., 1990-1994?]*

Stevens County Historical Society. *The Lookout cookbook: Region one.* [Colville, Wash.]: The Society, 1986, 1966.

Fiction and Poetry

Abbey, Edward. *Black Sun.* Santa Barbara: Capra Press, 1999.

Golding, Leila Prince. *Cynthia.* Minneapolis, Minn.: Bethany House, 1994.

Kerouac, Jack. *The Dharma Bums.* New York: Penguin Books, 1986.

Luke, Pearl. *Burning Ground.* New York: Plume Books, 2000.

Reece, Coleen L., and Albert B. Towne. *Crows'- Nests and Mirrors.* Uhrichsville, OH: Heartsong Presents, 1993.

Smith, Florence B. *Uncontained Fire.* Independence, Mo.: Two Trails Pub., 1998.

Snyder, Gary:

Riprap and Cold Mountain Poems. San Francisco: Grey Fox Press, 1958.
No Nature: New and Selected Poems. New York: Pantheon Books, 1992.
The Back Country. New York: New Directions, 1968.
Left Out in the Rain: New Poems, 1947-1985. San Francisco: North Point Books, 1986.

Wheeler, Ruth Carr. *Smoke in the Sky: a Story of a National Forest.* Mountain View, Calif.: Pacific Press Pub. Association, 1956.

Juvenile Fiction

Bunting, Eve, and Barry Moser. *On Call Back Mountain.* New York: Blue Sky Press, 1997.

Hatch, Judy. *The Dragonfly of Lookout Mountain*. Mount Shasta, Ca.: Earth Heart, 1996.

Pomeroy, Pete. *The Mallory Burn*. New York: Grosset & Dunlap, Inc., 1971.

Van Valkenburgh, Norman J., and Russell V. Van Valkenburgh. *Cub Scouts Climb the Tower: Hunter Mountain*, 1963. Fleischmanns, N.Y.: Purple Mountain Press, 2000.

Vail, Esther C. *Snow King Lookout*. Ginn and Company, 1964.

Wall, Cynthia, and Sheila Somerville. *Firewatch!* Newington, CT: American Radio Relay League, 1993.

History

Bates, Malcolm S. *Three Fingers: The Mountain, The Men and a Lookout*. 2nd revised edition. Seattle: Mountaineers, 1987.

Davies, Gilbert W. *Stories of the Klamath National Forest: The First 50 Years, 1905-1955*. Hat Creek, CA: HiStory Ink Books, 1992.

Greenfield, Marguerite. *The Old Fire Bell on Tower Hill*. [Helena, Mont.]: Landmarks Association, 1937.

Hayden, David and Martin Podskoch. *Adirondack Fire Towers: Their History and Lore: the Southern Districts*. Fleischmanns, N.Y.: Purple Mountain Press, 2003.

Hilton, David N. *From York to the Allagash: Forest Fire Lookouts of Maine 1905-1991*. Greenville, ME: Moosehead Communications, 1997.

Holland, Andy, and Cynthia Mallory. *Switchbacks*. Seattle: The Mountaineers, 1980

Keating, Linnea. *Fire Detection Lookout History on the Clearwater National Forest, Idaho*. Orofino, [Idaho]: U.S. Dept. of Agriculture, Forest Service, Northern Region, 1987

Kresek, Ray. *Fire lookouts of the Northwest*. Revised 3rd ed. Fairfield, Wash.: Ye Galleon Press, 1998.

Lorenz, David E.:

Fire Lookout Towers of the Grand Canyon. Flagstaff, Ariz.: The Author, 1998.

Tree Towers of the Grand Canyon. Flagstaff, Ariz.: [D.E. Lorenz], 1997.

Podskoch, Martin. *Fire Towers of the Catskills: their History and Lore.* Fleischmanns, N.Y.: Purple Mountain Press, 2000.

Reaves, Irma. *Lookouts of the Los Padres Forest.* [California, s.n.], 1988.

Rolph, J.W. *Former Fire Lookout Registry.* Glenwood, Wash.: J.W. Rolph, 1987.

Seattle (Wash.) Fire Department, Fire Prevention Division. *Fire Watch.* Seattle, WA: The Dept., 1999.

Spray, Richard H. *Jump-Off Joe Fire Lookout: old Cascadia Ranger District, Willamette National Forest.* [Oregon : R.H. Spray], 1998

Spring, Ira and Byron Fish. *Lookouts: Firewatchers of the Cascades and Olympics.* 2nd revised edition. Seattle: The Mountaineers, 1996.

Suiter, John. *Poets on the Peaks: Gary Snyder, Philip Whalen & Jack Kerouac in the North Cascades.* New York: Counterpoint, 2002.

United States Forest Service, Southwestern Region. *Lookouts in the Southwestern Region.* [Albuquerque, NM?]: USDA Forest Service, [1989].

Historic Preservation

Atwood, Katherine C. *Historic Fire Lookouts on the Siskiyou National Forest : Cultural Property Inventory and Request for a Determination of Eligibility to the National Register of Historic Places.* [Oregon]: Siskiyou National Forest, 1994.

Fire Lookout Towers: a Room with a View: Lassen National Forest, Hat Creek Ranger District. [Berkeley, Calif.?] : U.S. Dept. of Agriculture, Forest Service, Pacific Southwest Region, 1998.

Hartmans, Donna Marie. *Historic Lookout Stations on the Willamette National Forest: Management Plans for Preservation.* Thesis (M.A.), University of Oregon, 1991.

LaLande, Jeffrey M. *Dutchman Peak Lookout and Squaw Peak Lookout: Heritage Resource Evaluation and Rehabilitation Project Report.* Medford, Or.: Applegate Ranger District, Rogue River National Forest, 1998.

Laskey, Paul. *The Fire Observation Towers of New York State: Survivors that Still Stand Guard.* Ballston Spa, NY: MKL Publishers, 2003.

McLeod, Milo. *Lookouts on the Lolo National Forest.* [Missoula? Mont.: Lolo National Forest?, 1982?]

Morford, Lee. *Klamath National Forest and Siskiyou County Fire Lookouts, Fire Guard Stations.* [Yreka, Calif.: U.S. Forest Dept., 1980-1989?.]

Sinclaire, Elizabeth. *Historic Fire Lookouts on the Deschutes National Forest : a Determination of Eligibility to the National Register of Historic Places.* [Bend, Or.]: Deschutes National Forest, 1991.

Thornton, Mark V. *Fire lookouts of California: Historical Significance Evaluation.* [S.l.] : United States Department of Agriculture, Forest Service Region 5, 1987.

Thornton, Mark V. *An Inventory and Historical Significance Evaluation of CDF Fire Lookout Stations.* Sacramento, CA : The Office, 1993.

Williams, Gerald W. *An Inventory of the Known Lookout Locations in Western Oregon: Umpqua and Willamette National Forests.* [S.l. : s.n.], 1991.

Historic Works

Look-Out Tower: Camp Waskowitz. Seattle, Wash.: Highline Public Schools, 1900s.

Western Forestry and Conservation Association. *The Western Fire Fighter's Manual.* Portland, Ore., 1924.

New Jersey. Forest Fire Service. *Forest Firewardens.* [Trenton, N.J.]: Dept. of Conservation and Economic Development, State of New Jersey. 1900s.

Ramberg, Richard G. *Investigation of the Need and Feasibility of Improving Ground Detectors.* Missoula, Mont.: U.S. Dept. of Agriculture, Forest Service, Equipment Development Center, 1974.

Show, S.B. *Planning, Constructing, and Operating Forest-Fire Lookout Systems in California,* Washington, D.C.: U.S. Dept. of Agriculture, 1937.

United States. Forest Service. *Specifications and Plan for Lookout Towers,* 1924.

United States. Forest Service. *Specifications and Plans for Ready-Cut Lookout House.* [Washington, D.C.]: U.S. Dept. of Agriculture, Forest Service, 1924]

Oral Histories

Oral history interviews with lookouts are available at the K. Ross Toole Archives at the University of Montana –Missoula, the Idaho Oral History

Center at the Idaho State Historical Society in Boise, and the Library and Archives Department at the Montana Historical Society in Helena.

Travel Guides

Baird, Iris W., and Chris Haartz. *A Field Guide to New Hampshire Firetowers.* [Lancaster, N.H.?: I.W. Baird; New Hampshire Department of Resources and Economic Development, Forests and Lands, 1992.

Foley, Tom. *How to Rent a Fire Lookout in the Northwest: A Guide to Renting Fire Lookouts, Guard Stations, Ranger Cabins, Warming Shelters, and Bunkhouses in the National Forests of Oregon and Washington.* Wilderness Press, 1996.

Freeman, John P., and Wesley Haynes. *Views from on High: Fire Tower Trails in the Adirondacks and Catskills.* Lake George, N.Y.: Adirondack Mountain Club, 2001.

Gatesy, Carolyne Ilona. *Firetowers, Lookouts & Rustic Cabins for Rent: Northwest United States: California, Idaho, Montana, Nevada, Oregon, Utah, Washington, Wyoming.* Glastonbury, CT: Bear Mountain Press, 1997.

Look Out Guide for New Jersey. Trenton, NJ: Department of Conservation and Development, State of New Jersey, 1920-1929?.

Maine: Bureau of Forestry. *Maine Forest Service Fire Tower Visitor Information.* Augusta, Me.: Maine Forest Service [i.e. Bureau of Forestry], Dept. of Conservation, 1989.

Rustic Cabins & Lookouts of the Intermountain Region. Ogden, Utah: U.S. Dept. of Agriculture, Forest Service, Intermountain Region, 1993.

Websites

National Historic Lookout Register.
http://www.firetower.org/

Forest Fire Lookout Association.
http://www.firelookout.org/

Forest History Society.
http://www.lib.duke.edu/forest/

Rex s Fire Lookout Pages.
http://www.firelookout.com/

Recipe Notes

Order Form

Museum of North Idaho Publications Order Form

Name ______________________________
Address ____________________________
City _______________________________
State________ Zip __________________
Phone______________________________
e-mail _____________________________

QTY	TITLE	AMOUNT
___	PB *Bayview and Lakeview*	$14.95____
___	PB Dalton Story	$10.00____
___	SB From Hell to Heaven	$19.95____
___	PB In All The West	$24.95____
___	PB Idaho Minerals	$27.95____
___	PB Kootenai Chronicles	$10.00____
___	PB *Lookout Cookbook*	$14.95____
___	PB Milwaukee Road in Idaho	$19.95____
___	Hd Milwaukee Road Olympian	$39.95____
___	PB North Fork	$14.95____
___	PB Swiftwater People	$13.95____
___	Hd Swiftwater People	$23.95____
___	Hd Up The Swiftwater	$29.95____
___	PB Up The Swiftwater	$19.95____
___	Hd White Pine Route	$49.95____
___	PB Wildflowers of the Inland NW	$15.95____
___	Membership Dues	________

Subtotal ________
Members less 10% ______
Shipping ________

$4 shipping for the first book.
$1 for each additional book to the same address
Credit card orders can be taken at our website using Pay Pal. Go to www.museumni.org

Museum of North Idaho
P.O. BOX 812
Coeur d'Alene, ID 83816-0812
208-664-3448 e-mail: dd@museumni.org

Additional books are available at www.firelookout.org

Museum of North Idaho Photo and Archive Collection

The Museum of North Idaho is a non-profit organization committed to collecting, preserving and interpreting the history of the Coeur d'Alene region. The Idaho Panhandle National Forest donated archives and over 7,000 photographs relating to activities on the St. Joe, Coeur d'Alene and Kaniksu National Forests. This collection, as well as other information and photos relating to the history of Kootenai, Benewah and parts of Shoshone counties, is available to researchers by contacting the Museum of North Idaho at 208-664-3448 or info@museumni.org or visit www.museumni.org

The Mission of the Museum of North Idaho is to educate the community and visitors about the history of the Coeur d'Alene region.

*Implementation of this mission will give the community and its visitors an awareness, understanding and appreciation of the area's cultural heritage.

*A community that understands its past develops community pride, which leads to involvement and support of historical programs, projects and preservation.

*To achieve its mission, the Museum has a comprehensive collection of artifacts and materials that reflect the history of the area. The collection is preserved, exhibited and is available to the general public and researchers according to professional museum standards.